Glimpses of Christ in Everyday Lives

Karla Worley

New Hope Publishers
Birmingham, Alabama

New Hope Publishers
P.O. Box 12065
Birmingham, AL 35202-2065

Dewey Decimal Classification: 248.843
Subject Heading: Christian Life—Women

Cover design by Pamela Moore

ISBN: 1-56309-253-0
N984107 • 0598 • 5M1

To order products from New Hope Publishers or for a
free catalog, call 1-800-968-7301. Also, visit our Website
at **newhopepubl.com.**

This book is dedicated to my sister-in-law, Kim Cox. For many years, I prayed for you and walked with you until you came to Christ. Now you have become my precious sister! I thank you for the glimpses of Christ you give to me every single day. It is so obvious that He lives in you.

"I thank my God every time I remember you. I always pray with joy being confident of this, that he who began a good work in you will carry it on to completion until the day of Christ Jesus" (Phil. 1:3–6).

Contents

Many thanks are due to the women included in this book and to those who were not included. You opened your lives to me with such willingness and humility. You blessed me.

I owe a great deal to Susan Hansen, Cindy Dake, Laura Savage, and Andrea Mullins at Woman's Missionary Union® in Birmingham, Alabama, who entrusted me with this responsibility. You have encouraged, inspired, and empowered me from the first time I met you. I'm so thankful that God has placed you in my life.

Thank you to my copy editor, Leslie Caldwell, who came into this project midstream, but with much care and attention helped it stay true to its original vision.

Introduction

Am I Different?

Redeemed people make a difference
in an unredeemed world.
—Michael Glenn, pastor
Brentwood Baptist Church
Brentwood, Tennessee

When I was in the first grade, I became a Christian. On a Sunday night I walked down the aisle, took the preacher's hand and asked Jesus to live in my heart. I can still remember getting ready for school the next morning, looking in the mirror and wondering if my friends could tell by looking at me that I was different.

For many years after, I set about the business of churchmanship: Bible study, Sunday school, choir, missions activities, church camps, and Vacation Bible Schools. You name it: I memorized it, sang it, taught it, shared it, gave it, and prayed about it.

I also gossiped, envied, boasted, coveted, wounded, lied, over-committed my time, overspent my pocketbook, and generally blended into my world. I wasn't really different, except that I was very busy at church. I was living in the way the apostle Paul described the church at Corinth, "as mere man" (1 Cor 3:4). This is not how we were meant to live.

More than 35 years later, I have come

to understand that the six-year-old girl looking in the mirror had it right: Since Jesus now lives in my heart, I am different. And people ought to be able to see it not by my churchmanship, but by my character, my choices, and the quality of my everyday life. As Christ is formed more and more in me, my life should offer glimpses of Him to my world.

I am a product of the American church. I love the church. So I can say with understanding, yet great sadness, that I believe for the most part we have failed our calling to equip believers "to the measure of the stature which belongs to the fullness of Christ" (Eph 4:12–13). The vast majority of churches today are equipping their members either to fit into the Christian subculture or to blend in with the social culture.

No wonder we are confused. We are caught between two worlds: the Monday through Saturday maze of TV, internet, checkbooks, credit cards, car pools, classrooms, ball games, office politics, grocery lists, and shopping malls, and that Sunday "other-world" of religion. The two seem hardly to relate.

As Bob Briner writes in *Roaring Lambs*:

"Well, things are not even close to being perfect and to a certain extent, I do blame the church. For despite all the fancy buildings, sophisticated programs, and highly visible presence, it is my contention that the church is almost a nonentity when it comes to shaping culture. Culturally, we are lambs. Meek, lowly, easily dismissed cuddly creatures that are fun to watch but never a threat to the status quo.

It's time for those lambs to roar.

We feel we are making a difference because we are so important to ourselves. We have created a phenomenal subculture with our own media, entertainment, educational system and political hierarchy so that we have the sense that we're doing a lot. But what we've really done is create a ghetto that is easily dismissed by the rest of society."[1]

Today Christians aren't disturbing the world—at least not with our relevance and power. If anything, we entertain the world with our spats, baffle it with our inconsistency, and irritate it with our outreach methods.

This reminds me of another grade-school story I once heard. It seemed that one little boy, seized by evangelistic fervor, was trying his hardest to witness to the girl seated behind him. After enduring his outreach throughout one entire class, the little girl had enough and shouted, "Leave me alone! I am a Christian, you blockhead!"

Too many of us blockheads have rushed into the world with our techniques and formulas, hardly distinguishable from the sales pitches of soft drinks or Bob's Used Cars. Many Christians are confused and guilty about witnessing, because the methods offered seem unnatural and phony to us. We are right; they are phony. As Brennan Manning writes, "The gospel will persuade no one unless it has so convicted us that we are transformed by it."[2]

At the risk of seeming simplistic, let me offer a theory of evangelism that I believe was modeled by Christ and His followers in the early church: The most convincing way to witness to the power of Christ before unbelievers is to live among them and be different.

Let me say that again: The most convincing way to witness to the power of Christ before unbelievers is to live among them and be different.

Now, I didn't say "live among them and be weird." It's a lot easier to call everybody "brother" or paste a "Honk if you love Jesus" bumper sticker on your car. Jesus didn't call us to be salesmen, promoters, or peddlers.

"But you will receive power when the Holy Spirit comes on you; and you will be my witnesses" (Acts 1:8a).

Christ came "to testify to the truth" (John 18:37). It was in the everyday course of life that He gave this witness—a meal, a wedding, a well, a church meeting—ordinary places to which He gave new meaning by His presence. When Christ says, "Be my witnesses," He calls us to eat, work, and live in ordinary places, demonstrating a profound difference to the people we encounter because of Christ's presence in our lives.

Richard Foster wrote, "He Who is the Way shows us the way to live so that we increasingly come to share his love, hope, feelings, and habits. He agrees to be yoked to us, as we are yoked to Him, and to train us in how to live our lives as He would live them if he were in our place."[3]

Simply stated, there ought to be a discernible difference in the life of a believer and the life of an unbeliever. That difference is the presence of Jesus Christ. To the extent that He lives in us and transforms us, we will become more like Him and the world will see it. As Michael Green writes, "there is nothing so attractive in the world as a life where Jesus is dominant."[4]

You know and I know men and women whose lives are like that. Through them, Christ walks the halls of hospitals and grocery stores, teaches in classrooms, and manages corporations and countries. Through them, He sings, writes, dances, and acts. Through them, He loves, nurtures, empowers, breaks down barriers, and raises up standards. In this book, you will meet some women who live in that way. Not all have chosen Christian professions. All are very human. None would call themselves spiritual giants. But all of them share one distinctive: their lives bear the unmistakable signature of Jesus, the only explanation for their choices, character, and quality of life. They offer their world glimpses of Christ. Their examples are inspiring.

The good news is that because Christ lives in us, we have the potential to live such attractive and different lives. As my pastor, Mike Glenn, likes to remind us, "If God goes anywhere this week, it will be our feet that carry Him. If God says anything to anyone, it will be with our mouths. If God touches anyone, it will

be with our hands. And if He loves anyone, it will be with our hearts. We are
the body of Christ."

Manning wrote: "The greatest need of
our time is for the church to become
what it has seldom been: the body of
Christ with its face to the world, loving
others regardless of religion or culture,
pouring itself out in a life of service,
offering hope to a frightened world, and
presenting itself as a real alternative to
the existing arrangement."[5]

I am, after so many years, learning to
distinguish between churchmanship and
Christlikeness. I have spent the great part
of my life devoted to churchmanship; I
am resolved to spend the rest of my life
devoted to Christlikeness. I am like a
first-grader again, stretching to look in
the mirror each morning and wondering,
"Now that Jesus lives in my heart, can
people tell by looking at me that I am
different?"

Perhaps you would like to ask yourself
this question, too. If so, this book is for
you.

[1]Briner, Bob, *Roaring Lambs* (Grand Rapids: Zondervan, 1993),
27–29.

[2]Manning, Brennan, *The Signature of Jesus* (Sisters: Multnomah
Books, 1996), 17.

[3]Foster, Richard, "Becoming Like Christ," *Christianity Today* (5
Feb. 1996), 28.

[4]Green, Michael, *Evangelism Then & Now* (Downers Grove: Inter-
Varsity press. 1979), 52.

[5]Manning, 7.

1

The Key, The Door, The Cup

Here I am! I stand at the door and knock. If anyone hears my voice and opens the door, I will come in and eat with him, and he with me (Rev. 3:20).

When I was a child, a picture hung on the wall of my Sunday school classroom—a copy of a famous painting in which Jesus stands at the arched doorway of a small cottage, His hand raised to knock, His ear inclined to listen for a response. It is the artist's rendering of Revelation 3:20.

My Sunday school teacher used this painting to explain the process of becoming a Christian, or as she put it, "asking Jesus into your heart." This is how I have always pictured my life with Christ—the door of my heart opened to Him, He and I sitting at the kitchen table talking together. In fact, I wrote a lyric about it once:

"Right about now, I could use some glory. Right about now, I sure need some grace. Right about now, I wish we could sit down at this table where I could see You face to face. I wish I could pour You some coffee; I wish we could spend an hour, 'cause I could sure use some glory right about now."[1]

You know what? That's what He wants, too! On the night of His arrest, sitting around the table at the Passover meal, Jesus described this relationship to His disciples: "If anyone loves me, he will obey my teaching. My Father will love him, and we will come to him and make our home with him" (John 14:23).

Christ making His home in me—that's what it means to *ask Jesus into your heart.* Unfortunately, many of us hear Him knocking, open the door, and leave Him standing on the porch while we talk with Him. He never gets past the door.

Ever heard of *door people?* Door people are those who hear Christ knock and open the door to salvation, but they never go beyond; they sit down at the door. Door people like to sing door songs and tell door stories, reliving that wonderful moment when they opened the door. Salvation is a wonderful experience, but it is just the beginning. There is much more beyond it when Christ moves in and a relationship begins.

It might surprise you to know that this passage in Revelation was written not to nonbelievers, but as an invitation to the church. Laodicea was one of the wealthiest, most prosperous cities in the Roman Empire. Jesus' words to them in Revelation 3 indicate that the church had absorbed the attitude of the culture—smug, self-satisfied, and complacent to the point that He described them as *lukewarm.* Like a tepid cup of coffee, He wanted to spit them out.

Furthermore, said Jesus, these church members didn't even realize their condition. "You say, 'I am rich; I have acquired wealth and do not need a thing.' But you do not realize that you are wretched, pitiful, poor, blind and naked" (Rev. 3:17).

Jesus spoke to the church at Laodicea in the same way He spoke to the Pharisees, whom He called "blind guides" and "white-washed tombs full of dead man's bones" (Matt. 23:24,27)—all show on the outside, nothing on the inside. By contrast, Acts describes the first believers in Jerusalem as people whose lives were radically transformed: "They devoted themselves to the apostles' teaching and to the fellowship, to the breaking of bread and to prayer. Everyone was filled with awe, and many wonders and miraculous signs were done by the apostles. All the believers were together and had everything in common. Selling their possessions and goods, they gave to anyone as he had need. Every day they continued to meet together in the temple courts. They broke bread in their homes and ate together with glad and sincere hearts, praising God and enjoying the favor of the people" (Acts 2:42–47a).

These were the same people who had been cowering in an upper room only weeks before, bickering for first place in the kingdom, unsure about when it would come, afraid for their lives when it did. This transformation was a mystery to the people around them. Were they

drunk? Had they lost their minds? Acts 4
tells us that even the Jewish leaders
"were astonished and they took note
that these men had been with Jesus"
(Acts 4:13).

What the world needs are believers
whose daily lives cannot be explained
apart from the presence of the irre-
sistible and unmistakable Christ. The
daily lives of the early believers were
convincing proof that He now lived in
them. In Antioch, this was so evident
that believers were first given the name
Christiani, meaning *little Christs*. What
Jesus had promised had come true:
although He was not with them in physical form, His presence was still undeni-
able. Note the result: "And the Lord
added to their number daily those who
were being saved" (Acts 2:47*b*).

The Laodicean believers did not see
themselves as they really were: empty.
They did not see where Christ actually
stood in their church: *outside* the door.
Without Him, they were unable to fulfill
their purpose. The same is true for us.

The women you will meet in this
book have one thing in common: at
some point in their lives, they realized
that they were spiritually bankrupt, an
empty shell, all outside and no inside.
They had heard Jesus' voice, but left
Him standing on the doorstep. Each of
them can point to a moment when they
opened the door of their lives to Him
and invited Him to live there. They have
built a relationship with Him, and they
all say they cannot live without it.

The Key

As my Sunday School teacher pointed out to us, there is no handle on the door in the painting. It must be opened from the inside. In my mind's eye, I imagined there must be a key. The key is God's Word. It is what unlocks our hearts and minds. "The word of God is living and active. Sharper than any double-edged sword, it penetrates even to dividing soul and spirit, joints and marrow; it judges the thoughts and attitudes of the heart" (Heb. 4:12).

God knows the areas of our lives where we have closed the door to Him and locked it. When He speaks to us through His Word, a light comes on. We see how empty a room is when we have not allowed Him into it. His Word is the key He has given to us to unlock the door. We don't have to be whitewashed tombs. Jesus said: "The words I have spoken to you are spirit and they are life" (John 6:63b).

The Door

Each person reading this book has a locked door somewhere in her life—a place where she has not allowed Christ to go. Which door have you locked against Christ? Perhaps it is your place of business, or a relationship. Perhaps you have not allowed Him into your past, or into your plans for the future. It may be your bank account or your leisure time. In those areas, you might, like the Laodiceans, consider yourself "just fine." In fact, you may even look

just fine on the outside. Don't be fooled,
Christ says.

We cannot transform ourselves. We
can rearrange the furniture, throw a few
slipcovers over shabby things, white-
wash the walls, but only Christ can do
the work of reconstructing us into His
image. It is a big job, and He works
room by room. He will hand us the key,
but it is we who must fling wide the
door and say, "Make Yourself at home."

The Cup

"If anyone hears my voice and opens
the door, I will come in and eat with
him, and he with me" is Jesus' promise
in Revelation 3:20*b*. In the ancient
world, sharing a meal with someone
was more than sharing food; it was a
symbol of affection and intimacy. Christ
used this custom to explain the intimacy
of His relationship to the believer. "Take
and eat; this is my body…This is my
blood of the covenant which is poured
out for many for the forgiveness of sins"
(Matt. 26:26,28).

To sit down with Christ at the table is
to share that kind of intimacy—to know
each other's hearts and minds, to be as
close as one body and one blood. We
get to share the cup of fellowship—to
talk with Christ, to know He is close, to
hear Him speak, to share our joys, and
to share His triumphs. It is also the cup
of suffering.

The mother of disciples James and
John once came to Jesus to ask that her
sons be able to sit right next to Jesus in

His coming kingdom (Matt. 20:20,23*a*). "You don't know what you are asking," Jesus said to them. "Can you drink the cup I am going to drink?"

"We can," they answered.

"You will indeed drink from my cup," Jesus said. He knew that the disciples would face the same suffering He did—persecution, danger, even death. To sit close to Christ is not a warm, cozy coffee klatch. The apostle Paul understood that; he understood the cost of inviting Christ into his life. From prison he wrote: "I want to know Christ and the power of his resurrection and the fellowship of sharing in his sufferings" (Phil. 3:10).

It is possible to walk along with Jesus for a long time and not truly know Him or understand His words. That's what happened to two disciples on the road to Emmaus, the very day of Jesus' resurrection (Luke 24:13–35). It was not until they sat down at the table with Jesus that they recognized Him and truly knew He was alive. It is not until we share the cup, partaking intimately with Him in friendship, obedience, and experience, that He is revealed.

An Invitation

In this book, you will find notes in the margins. They are meant to draw you into the conversation, and to help you unlock the doors in your heart where Christ is still waiting to be welcomed.

Often during the writing of this book, as I talked with one of the women interviewed, a Scripture would come to mind. I have notated them in the margin, indicated by the *key symbol.*

That key may just fit a door in your heart. Questions in the margins will help you think about the areas of your life where you need to open the door to Christ. These questions are indicated by the *door symbol.*

Finally, Christ offers you an invitation: Take this cup. Listen carefully as God tells you how you can cooperate with what He is doing in your life. Write it down in the space marked at the end of each chapter with the *symbol of the cup.*

Each of the women you are about to meet graciously opened the door of her life to me. We talked openly about our struggles, shortcomings, and God's sufficiency. They showed me what God has done in their everyday, ordinary, sleeping, eating, going-to-work, walking-around lives. I did not meet them all face-to-face; many of us chatted by email, some by fax. Often we met over our coffee cups by telephone late at night. Walking through the corridors of their hearts, I saw glimpses of Christ.

Their open invitation is extended to you. Imagine that you have pulled up a chair and joined us. Bring your coffee cup; find a quiet corner. I guarantee that when our conversation is done, you will say, "They have been with Jesus."

[1] "Right About Now," Lyrics by Karla Worley (©1997 Word Music/ASCAP). Used by permission. All rights reserved.

2

Incarnation

Becoming the Face of God

*The Word became flesh and lived for a
while among us. We have seen his glory,
the glory of the one and only Son, who
came from the Father, full of grace
and truth* (John 1:14).

There is an old preacher's story about a
little boy who could not sleep in his
own room because he was afraid of
being alone in the dark. Night after
night, he called for a parent to come
and sleep with him. On one such night,
the boy's mother assured him that he
was never alone. "God is right here with
you," she said.

"I know that," replied the boy, "but I
need somebody with skin on him."

On the night Christ was born in a tiny
stable in Bethlehem, God put skin on
and "lived among us," as John described
it. Even the baby's name, Emmanuel,
means *God with us.* This is what the
theological term *incarnation* means:
God took on a human form. He ate
with us, touched us, talked to us.

One of the disciples' greatest fears
was that Jesus would indeed leave
them, as He predicted. Then what? Who
would be God in human skin? Jesus'
answer: "You will."

"I will put my Spirit in you," God promised through the prophet Ezekiel (Eze. 36:27*a*). Jesus completed this promise when He said, "I will ask the Father, and he will give you a Counselor ...the Spirit of truth...for he lives with you and will be in you" (John 14:16*a*,17). People still need a God who is here with them. Through the Holy Spirit, He now wears our skin: incarnation.

Linda Knott

When I called Linda Knott to ask for an interview, a friendly, out-of-breath voice answered the phone, "Woodcock Baptist Center!"

"Is Linda in?" I asked, thinking I'd have to go through a secretary or assistant to get to the Center's director.

"This is Linda!" she laughed.

"Are you busy?" I asked.

"Yes!" she answered. "I'm serving lunch. Can you call me back in about 30 minutes?"

For nearly 30 years, Linda Knott has served in some capacity at the Woodcock Baptist Mission Center, located in the Cayce government housing community of Nashville, Tennessee. She has volunteered in the Woodcock Christmas Toy Store, taught nutrition under the University of Tennessee extension program, managed a day-care program and Wednesday soup kitchen, a women's ministry, clothing room, food pantry, and supervised the work of student summer missionaries, including Back Yard Bible Clubs, youth picnics, Vacation Bible School, and door-to-door evangelism. She has truly become the face of God to this inner-city area of Nashville.

When we finally had the opportunity to talk, I asked about her spiritual journey.

Linda, you have such a servant's heart. How long have you been serving Christ by ministering to others?

When I was 15½ years old, I accepted Christ. One week later, I surrendered to service—literally! I heard about missionaries; I understood they were people who told others about Jesus. I wanted to do that.

"On the side of Woodcock Center is a painting of Jesus with His arms outstretched to children. Every day, addicts and alcoholics in this neighborhood walk past our building and around the corner to buy their liquor or crack, and they see that invitation: Come unto Me.

"The reason that government programs or GEDs don't work is that they don't have the power to change lives, just outward circumstances. You can give a family a bag of groceries, but that only fills their stomachs for a week. It doesn't provide them with what they need to be a healthy family. That's what Jesus was talking about when He said to the woman at the well, 'Everyone who drinks this water will be thirsty again,

"Let the little children come to me, and do not hinder them, for the kingdom of God belongs to such as these. I tell you the truth, anyone who will not receive the kingdom of God like a little child will never enter it" (Mark 10:14–15).

What childlike qualities allow a person to be open to Christ?

but whoever drinks the water I give him will never thirst' (John 4:13). Yes, I am an advocate of practical ways to meet human need, but at some point we must meet the need that is in their hearts in order to truly help them. So, on Wednesdays we provide lunch, sacks of groceries, and a worship service.

"There are great opportunities right now for the church to take its place in the community. In Tennessee prisons, funding for education was cut recently; there is only one teacher provided. The government is abdicating its responsibilities for education and social reform. I see this as a good thing! We are putting together a list of volunteers who have teaching experience. The church now has an open door, and we are the ones who can really change lives by being Christlike in a prison setting. To be Christlike means that the Christ Who came to indwell me at salvation is the Christ Who compels me into the world."

I love Eugene Peterson's translation of Romans 15:2–3 in The Message*:*

"Strength is for service, not status. Each one of us needs to look after the good of the people around us, asking ourselves, 'How can I help?' That's exactly what Jesus did. He didn't make it easy for himself by avoiding people's troubles, but waded right in and helped out. 'I took on the troubles of the troubled,' is the way Scripture puts it."

It's so hard to get people to under-stand that they don't experience the joy of their salvation until they give it away. For one thing, you call on Him more!"

No kidding! I learned that on my first overseas volunteer missions trip, where I lived and worked in a government hous-ing project similar to this one. At the beginning of the trip, I was praying for myself mostly—but by the end of the trip, I was praying for the people around me. I realized how petty most of my prayers were once I got out on the front lines.

Yes, true revival comes out of pray-ing for and serving others. I have summer missionaries come here to work, and it does more for them than they do for others! By the end of the summer, they're in a spiritual fervor. It changes them."

Is that why many of us are afraid to leave the pew and go out, because it might change us?

Sure. It will cost us something. We can't be complacent anymore. I had to give up church to follow Christ—liter-ally! Sunday night is my favorite time at church; it's family time. But it was the time that was available to me to begin a ministry at the women's prison. I had to make a choice."

"Restore to me the joy of your salvation" (Psalm 51:12).

Do you remember how you felt when you were saved? Tell your testimony to someone.

"Any of you
who does not
give up every-
thing he has
cannot be my
disciple" (Luke
14:33).

Is God calling
you to some-
thing specific?
What will you
have to give up
in order to fol-
low Him?

So you gave up what was comfortable.

My mentor, Mrs. C.D. Creasman, used to say, 'I just hope and pray I'm as good a follower of Christ as I am a Southern Baptist.' You have to adjust your life to God. As Henry Blackaby says, accepting God's invitation to join Him in His work precipitates a crisis of belief that requires major adjustments.[1] Some of the finest people I know are the real believers at the women's prison. They have nothing else to cling to but Him. We have so much to let go of. When people turn loose of their lives and accept Christ's call, it means radical change."

Radical? But not everyone will be called to the same sacrifice. Not everyone gets led to full-time missions.

No! We need people in the church, too. I wouldn't be who I am if not for leaders and teachers who equipped me. That's the job of the church—to equip. I've had a lot of good training by serving in almost every area of the church.

"I've also been trained for ministry by a major illness that put me completely on my back. I learned a lot during that time. Teenagers I worked with at church would come to see me and bring their friends to my house—friends who would never come to church! We would talk about their lives, their problems. Some of these girls came to know Christ during that time. I'll tell you what I learned: for me to do Christ's work, I just have to be a willing vessel."

Yes! I sometimes think I need to organize a program, a committee, a budget, identify my talents, my spiritual gifts— that God needs all that to accomplish something. He doesn't; He just needs me to show up and be available. Just showing up—being there—is the big part of my responsibility!

I've learned to avoid my *gift of persuasion.* I don't try to persuade anyone to come to Christ; but if they ask me, I'll tell them about Christ! I worked with some of those girls for three years—and bit my tongue the whole time!"

Sitting on folding chairs in that concrete-floored room of the mission center, Linda introduced me to a new concept: the principle of incarnation—planting your life among others.

For many years, I wanted to start a Bible study group for women in this area. I tried several times, but had no success. Then I watched friends Art and Diane Sheppard, who moved in right across the street from here. Diane put her life here; she is one of the women in the area. She shops where they shop, hangs her laundry in the back yard, and plays with their children. She has started

"But we have this treasure in jars of clay to show that this all–surpassing power is from God and not from us" (2 Cor. 4:7).

Think about your life. What are the places where you could just "show up" and be a willing vessel? Can you relinquish your need to "do something"?

"For God, who said, 'Let light shine out of darkness,' made his light shine in our hearts to give us the light of the knowledge of the glory of God in the face of Christ" (2 Cor. 4:6).

Who has been the face of Christ to you?

a Bible study in her home, and they come. Incarnation works!"

In August 1997, Linda Knott retired as director of Woodcock Baptist Mission Center. The Center's future is uncertain. Linda's prayer is that churches in the area will see the opportunity to be the face, hands, and feet of Jesus to this community where over 150 doors are open to visitation and cultivation. But church members will have to leave their comfortable pews and get out among the people. They will have to plant their lives there.

In the future, I see a radical church evolving—a shake-up. Models for new churches have come out of groups who have come here to volunteer. They go home and abandon new building programs. Instead, they buy a storefront and go into ministry. There is no church building; there are people being trained for ministry. The church exists for service. We exist to be the face of Jesus Christ."

What does the face of Jesus look like? Maybe it's not just your average well-dressed churchgoer. The church of Jesus' time thought He would look like a prophet, or a ruler, but He looked like a carpenter. The face of Christ today may be a doctor, a teacher, an old man, or a

child. Or He may have red hair and freckles, drive a Jeep, and walk the halls of the local high school.

Eve Sarrett

Eve Sarrett likes to say she grew up pagan. She explained to me why.

My mother grew up in the Church of Christ; my Dad, Episcopalian. When they married, they decided that neither church was where they wanted to raise their children, so they settled on a Presbyterian church until we were old enough to say, 'I don't want to go'—and they succumbed to our power, because they weren't committed either. So, probably by the time I was nine years old, I started staying home. My parents were very moral; good citizenship, perfect attendance in school—all that was ingrained. But it was apart from any kind of relationship with God."

During Eve's sophomore year in high school, Young Life, a Christian organization for teenagers, began at a neighboring school.

All the older guys that I had crushes on went to Young Life.[2] Part of the organization's strategy is to get some of the key kids involved, because they know others will follow. And we did.

"No one can come to me unless the Father who sent me draws him" (John 6:44).

Who is a "sponge" in your life?

"I can remember the first club I went to, being pulled up front and put in a skit. For my personality, that was not an offensive thing, that was a 'Yeah! I'm already being noticed!' I remember hearing for the first time about Jesus as somebody who seemed relate-able. I was attracted."

"Relateable" is exactly the word to describe Eve Sarrett. She is a magnet for teenage girls. That's how her group called Pancakes and Parables began.

Our Youth Director asked me to teach a group during a Disciple Now weekend. I ended up not just teaching, but hosting the group at our house. And when I got in with that group of girls, I offered, "Come over to my house. We'll study the Bible." Every other Saturday they come to my house, and I'm a short order cook; they come in and I generally give them two kinds of pancakes to choose from. And they say nobody makes 'em like I do."

Teenagers get up on a Saturday morning to study the Bible?

Yeah! These kids are sponges waiting to soak up stuff."

Were you?

The spring of my sophomore year in high school, I had a well-intentioned but militant Christian worker corner me in the mall and share with me the four spiritual laws. And I repeated what she said, not for the purpose of faith, but to get rid of her. Two months later, I was going to Young Life camp in North Carolina. In unveiling the gospel, they have a progression: 'Is there a God, and if so what does He look like?' Follow that with the claims of Christ. And then, 'Who are we?' We are sinners, apart from God—hopeless, helpless. But God did something about it; He sent Jesus to die on the cross. Finally, 'What does it mean to be a Christian; how do you become a Christian?' It was a low-pressure, if not no-pressure, situation. They give you about 20 minutes to go off by yourself and think about what the speaker said and respond if you wish. I did.

"The difference between the mall "conversion" and this one was that my life changed. My Young Life leader used to say, 'A Christian is someone who turns out to be one.' I started to shave off parts of my life that didn't belong, that weren't godly. That was, I believe, the evidence that there was something different."

There's a danger for those of us who accept Christ as children and grow up in church: the Christian life becomes a cultural thing. We don't understand that we

"Therefore if anyone is in Christ, he is a new creation; the old has gone, the new has come!" (2 Cor. 5:17).

*must immediately make changes inter-
nally that lead us to live differently. I
was 30 before I started to figure that out!*

But if you look at the disciples for
instance, long before they accepted
Christ, they were following Him. During
their three years with Him, they didn't
get it—up to the very last minute! Most
of us have flipped those steps and said,
'You have to believe before you follow.'
I think a large part of the journey in
coming to believe is the wooing
process. To get to know Jesus, you've
got to be around His people.

"Being with other Christians is crucial,
too: I got plugged into a Bible study
right away and started reading the Bible
for myself—having somebody who was
older than me in the faith teach me how
to do stuff like read the verses in the
middle and cross-reference on my own."

*Is that how you were drawn into Bible
study?*

Oh, yeah. Immediately I felt called. I
didn't think there was an option. I
wanted other kids in my school to
know what I knew. We didn't have
Young Life at my school, and I bugged
the area director a zillion times: 'We've
got to have Young Life at my school.'
By my senior year, we did. I was immediately one of the people rounding up
kids saying, 'You gotta come to this, it's
cool. See who can swallow goldfish.' It
wasn't, 'Come hear about Jesus' so

much; it was, 'You won't believe how crazy these people are.'"

Exactly! The first summer our Youth Minister, Jay Austin, took our group on a missions trip, we held Backyard Bible Clubs in a trailer park in Greenville, Mississippi. Jay completely floored us by whipping out his guitar and doing a horrible Elvis imitation. What a goofball! But the children loved it, and he had them in the palm of his hand.

The apostle Paul said, "I have become all things to all men so that by all possible means I might save some" (1 Cor. 9:19–23). I guess I'll become a goldfish swallower if that means I'll get you there to listen to Christ.

That's right. That's why I go to high school basketball games and football games. If that's my target group, I've got to be there with them. I drive a car that most of them think is cool. I wear clothes that I wouldn't walk into certain tea parties in, but that's me; and it's not something that is offensive to them. I have a glass door on the front of my house. And when I leave the wood door open, and you drive by, I am saying, 'I am home, I am here for you and you can stop by.' So it's not unusual for one of them to walk in. What I pray now is that my son Cam and daughter McCall will have someone like me when they grow up, because I won't be cool to them."

"I have become all things to all men so that by all possible means I might save some" (1 Cor. 9: 19–23).

List all the kinds of people you encounter in daily life. How could you relate to them in order to build a basis for sharing the Gospel?

Does it work with your kids? Same principle?

O h, yeah—living among them, not necessarily lecturing them about the things of God. Just living it out in front of them. For instance, we have a big house and because I feel guilty about having a big house, I always have to have somebody live with me. This year we have a girl living with us, a senior at Baylor who dates a boy from here. (The trade-off is I get free baby-sitting—not a bad deal!) I'm a member of the YMCA. I'm right there by it, and it makes sense that she should be able to use it. So I called up the director, and I said that my niece was living with me. 'Would it be all right if she was part of our membership?'

"The director said, 'Sure, how do you spell her last name?' Well, I didn't know! I didn't know any of these things you should know about your own niece. And within half a second after I hung up the phone, the Holy Spirit was all over me. What I had done was wrong.

"I wrestled with it all the way from my playroom to my bedroom, and then I knew I was going to get busted because Jason, her boyfriend, is a member of the Y. As soon as she walked in with him, they'd say, 'Oh, you're Eve's niece.' So that was enough guilt and condemnation to call the director back and say, 'Are you going to be there awhile?' I knew that the first conversation was okay over the phone but the second one needed to be in her office.

"I went to her and said, 'I lied. I just totally flat-out lied.' And she said, 'I'm so glad!'

"I said, 'No, no, let me confess. Lindsay's not my niece, but she does live with us.'

"She said, 'Well I just told somebody today that there are still people in the world like you that are honest and trustworthy.'

"I said, 'But you don't understand—I'm not! Did you not hear me?' I can't live like that. Truth is truth."

There's your incarnation: Cam and McCall are seeing a quality of Christ lived out right before them in their mother.

I think it's a compliment that Camden and McCall were sitting in church and Cam drew a picture of me. At the top he wrote 'Bible Woman,' and he drew a Bible around my hands with a cross on it. But I haven't made him study the Bible with me. I'm taking the approach of living among them."

Living among them can sometimes take you far away from home. Like many people, I am in awe of missionaries who pack up and move to the other side of the

world. As I have come to know many of them, I have learned that this is not necessarily the huge leap I imagine it would be. Often, God has already planted their hearts there long before He plants their lives. When that happens, halfway-around-the-world can be "home."

Julie Poe

The cereal bowls are barely washed when it starts. The phone rings. "I need help in filling out my job application." "I need to buy a computer; what do I do? How do I pay on time?" "Can you help set up English classes?" Paul Poe answers patiently, repeating himself often.

His wife, Julie, is busy putting things into the ever-expanding pack she seems to be attached to. Several mornings a week she loads up, walks the six blocks to the New York City subway and heads for China Town, about an hour ride away. Winding through the crowds of chattering, pushing, rushing people, she stops on a side street and steps into a tiny space to catch the elevator up to the third floor of a garment factory. She is greeted with a cheery "Hello, Teacher!" Piles of brightly colored satin and trim are heaped on the floors. Huge pots of rice are cooking against one wall. Dozens of workers are finishing up the few minutes before lunch break. They have tiny work areas and do the same thing over and over, sometimes for eleven hours a day. Julie teaches the women citizenship and English as a second language. They want very much to learn and they love their teacher, who also loves and encourages them.

Julie's parents described her life and environment in New York in a journal entry: "A short subway ride away, another world awaits. On the 78th floor of the World Trade Center are the offices of the Commercial Bank of Taiwan, where Julie teaches English and American culture to the bank president and other workers. Soon she will begin another afternoon of classes for their wives. God is loving all these people through Julie. Little by little, they will learn that, and it will be even more important than what they study today."

Julie, how did an Amarillo, Texas girl get to New York City?

I have known for a long time that there was a 'New York City?' uttered somewhere along the way deep inside me, and that I had said, 'Yes,' not knowing whether I was saying yes to a two-week missions trip or to a lifetime. I finally moved here in 1990, after teaching public school for one year near Amarillo. I fell in love with New York easily. But I returned to Texas for a year of studies at George W. Truett Seminary in Waco, Texas. After nine months, I was desperate for a way to get back to New York. I worked out a plan to serve as a summer/semester missionary for the

"Whether you turn to the right or to the left, your ears will hear a voice behind you, saying, 'This is the way; walk in it.'" (Isa. 30:21).

What do you know for sure that you have heard God utter inside of you?

"I am grieved that I have made Saul king, because he has turned away from me and has not carried out my instructions" (1 Sam. 15:9–11).

Selective obedience is disobedience. What is the hardest thing God could ask you to do? Would you do it?

Metropolitan New York Baptist Association and accomplish my requirements for seminary at the same time. Soon after I arrived that summer, I met Paul Poe, who had just graduated from Golden Gate seminary and was in New York for a church planting project. He needed to learn how to teach English as a second language because the neighborhood he was working in was 70 percent Spanish-speaking. So, his supervisor told him to contact me. He did, and we spent the summer and fall getting to know each other and working together on most of our ministry projects. That December, we were married in New York."

Did you always know you wanted to work in ministry?

When I was about fourteen, I was standing in my church singing the words to the hymn, 'Trust and Obey.' I was overwhelmed by how true I knew that would be for me. I understood at that moment that my whole life had to be one of serving God, or I could not possibly be satisfied. Some people would say that I made a commitment to 'special service' at that point, but I didn't make a public decision, and I didn't feel that I was being called to a particularly 'special' life. I believed—and I still do believe—that the way I was called to live my life, with trust and obedience in all things, is appropriate for every Christian."

*You realize, don't you, that you're
going to scare my readers to death!
That's exactly what we're all afraid of:
that your level of trust and obedience is
the norm expected of us—and that if we
get that serious, God will call us to New
York City or some other place way out of
our comfort zone!*

It's funny where different people's
comfort zones are. During my last bit
of college, I remember my roommate
asking me one day as we washed
dishes, 'What is the hardest thing God
could ask you to do with your life?'

"I thought for just a few minutes and
said, 'To go back to Amarillo, teach
ninth grade English, get married, have
2.5 children and a dog, join the PTA,
and teach Sunday School.'

"She said, 'Really? That would be
harder than say, Africa?'

"I said, 'For me right now, yes.'

"She asked, 'And if you felt that was
exactly what God was calling you to do
this fall, would you do it?'

"And I said, with little hesitation, 'Yes.'

"So, of course, you know where I was
that fall—not in New York, not in Africa,
not in some innovative, multicultural
big-city school. I was in a ninth grade
English room on the edge of Amarillo,
in a little school that was rumored to
have one non-white student (whom I
never saw).

"I remember the day of my interview
that August. I stood alone in my parent's house, crying and crying and

saying, 'Are you sure, God?' He seemed
to be sure, and my answer was still
'Yes.' I remember that during the week
of preparations before school began, I
kept discovering new little atrocities (in
my opinion): my classroom was completely lined with these horribly bright
orange bookshelves, *Romeo and Juliet*
was not in the textbook, and so on.
Each time I made a new discovery, I
would look up at God and say, 'Upping
the cost, huh?'

"There were, of course, good reasons
for me to be there that year. But within
two weeks after school was out that
spring, I was headed for New York. And
that's where I found my comfort zone. I
belong here in a way I never ever
belonged in Texas."

*Did that come from God? Did He
cause you to fall in love with New York?*

I remember the day when I really
sensed that love as more than a
tourist's enjoyment. It was during my
second month here. My friend had
taken me to the Cloisters, a lovely
medieval museum in the northern tip of
Manhattan. He suggested we take the
bus down to the midtown restaurant
where we would eat. It would be about
an hour's trip, but I would get to see a
lot of the city. It was captivating for me.
We went through very nice neighbor-
hoods, past lovely parks and ornate
cathedrals. We went through Harlem. As
you pass through the streets, you can

see the people groups change completely from one section to the next: Orthodox Jews here, Puerto Ricans here, African Americans there. My heart suddenly felt as if it would burst because I realized I cared about all of those people!

"Because it was so intense, I knew what I was experiencing was God's love for them and not just my own. I agreed at that time that I would be a channel for His love for this city. I am still consistently overwhelmed by the intensity and the stubbornness of that love."

Are you ever afraid, especially in dealing with homeless people and drug addicts?

I adopted a maxim fairly early in my life here: 'Careful, but not afraid.' I stay aware; I generally sense very quickly when I am in a place that is not particularly safe, and I just walk out purposefully and prayerfully. In a city where it is generally necessary to go about in a state of heightened awareness (for safety's sake), I have found over the years that that level of attention makes it easier for me to also have a heightened awareness of God's perspective of my situation."

How do you know what He would do? How do you know when to help and when to say no?

"He who belongs to God hears what God says. The reason you do not hear is that you do not belong to God" (John 8:47; 10:26–27).

Is there some area of your life in which you do not hear God? What barriers have you put up between you and Him?

Jesus promised that as one of His sheep, I know His voice (John 10:14,27). It is that simple—and that hard: I *know*. If I listen to His voice, rather than to my fears and the opinions of others, I know. As for our homeless friends, they soon figure out that we are Christians whether we say so directly or not, and they often even introduce us to other Christians in the neighborhood! We also generally ask to pray with them when they express great needs to us. *Great needs*—that sounds funny doesn't it, since I guess all of a homeless life looks like a great need to us! But there are still degrees of need: the need for a cup of coffee doesn't compare with the news that you're HIV-positive.

"My choices day to day seem to be simple: In this particular situation, will I behave as Christ would, or not? Sometimes, I don't even realize that I have made choices based on my own selfishness until hours later. Sometimes, I must admit that I see the choice clearly and allow my own fears or desire for comfort to win out. Sometimes, I see a need and try to meet it as Christ would, even though my heart secretly wishes this choice had not come my way at all. And sometimes, I see the moment as a precious opportunity to be the hands and feet and mouth and ears of Jesus in this place, and I rejoice even as I am choosing to be like Him."

Julie just described my own life perfectly. It is so simple, and so hard: in this particular situation, will I behave as Christ would, or not? My situations involve children, neighbors, grocery store clerks, church members; hers happen to include homeless people and internationals. It doesn't matter where you live, the choice is the same. And despite how different Julie's environment is from mine, the situations she describes are similar: whether to deal with an interruption in my busy schedule; whether to simply be kind.

Yesterday, I was on my way to church. I had a long wait for the first subway, so I kept looking at my watch and calculating how I would be able to do all that I needed to do. Before the service, I had to make copies of the bulletin and fold them. I also needed to meet with our pianist and song leader. When I arrived at 59th Street, where I had to transfer to a different subway, I was feeling a bit tense. Then I had to wait again.

"An older Russian woman was pacing nearby me. She was obviously more pained than I was by the delay. After each announcement over the intercom, she would come to me and ask what the buzz-blurred voice had said. I explained each time. Finally, after about ten minutes, she explained that she was feeling sick and needed a rest room badly. (The one in the subway station

"A priest happened to be going down the same road, and when he saw the man, he passed by on the other side" (Luke 10:30–37).

Are you too busy to stop for someone who needs you? Are you afraid to help?

was closed for repairs.) We waited a few more minutes, and then I said, 'I'm sure there is something nearby. Let's go.' So we exited the subway station and looked around. We saw a family pizza shop that was open, so we headed for it. She said, 'You ask? They no understand me.' I glanced at my watch and realized the musicians would be waiting for me. But I felt that I had been granted a chance to re-enact the Good Samaritan story, and asked myself which role I would play. So I waited and helped her get back to the right subway, where she left me with abundant thanks, hugs, and kisses.

"Another day, I was sitting on the subway in the evening rush hour, grateful to have a seat since I was quite tired. I noticed that an empty seat remained across the aisle from me, and wondered why. Then I realized that the empty seat was next to a man who was obviously homeless. He started to eye the big bag of bananas that a small Asian man in a suit was holding next to me. Then the homeless man began talking about bananas—how much he loved bananas, how good just one of those bananas would taste to him just then. I was wishing I had a banana to give him!

"Finally after several minutes of the banana monologue, my neighbor reached into his bag and handed a banana across the aisle. He managed to do so without ever making eye contact with the homeless man. Oh, how the homeless man thanked him and raved

about how delicious that banana was! I
decided that I was in a fairly safe position with so many passengers around,
so I caught his eye and smiled to let
him know that I appreciated his appre-
ciation.

"Then he addressed me directly, 'Do
you know what would be my idea of
perfection right now?' He looked me in
the eye, grinning all the time and said,
'To take a nice hot bath, mix up some
kind of great cold banana shake, and
then sit in front of a television all night
watching old movies. Wow! That's all I
could ever want!'

"I was taken aback by the simplicity
of his wish and by his enthusiasm in
describing it. We spent the next few
minutes discussing the best recipe for
his banana shake, raising our voices
over the noise and peering around
standing passengers. The strangest thing
happened then. It was as if he suddenly
became visible to the other people in
the subway. Someone filled the seat
next to him without a second thought. A
few others jumped into our discussion
with their own additions to the recipe.
As I got off at my stop, of course I
wished that I could take him home to
fulfill his wish. However, I had neither
the money for the shake ingredients nor
a TV for him to watch. So I left him
with a smile and an agreement to try
out that recipe sometime. And that was
enough. His face was brighter, and his
shoulders had lost their slump."

"This is to my Father's glory, that you bear much fruit, showing yourselves to be my disciples" (John 15:8).

Where has God planted you? Are you blooming?

Kindness. God on a subway—incarnation. What distinguishes you from a social worker, Julie? What makes it ministry?

A few years back, I was teaching about 60 hours a week in an entirely Chinese English-as-a second language school. I taught more than 100 students each week and had no time or energy to spend outside of class deepening relationships to the point where I could share Jesus verbally.

"A friend commented, 'So it's not enough for them to die and go to hell speaking perfect English?'

"Wow. I've never been able to walk away from that question. I still insist on being the best English teacher I can be in each situation. But I am convinced that what my students are attracted to is a deeper need than English. I really believe that consciously or unconsciously, they are looking for Jesus."

What quality of Jesus would you say is most significant for them to see in you?

M ercy, compassion…being approachable. Living in New York City really spotlights the fact that these are qualities of Christ, not of the world. The goal of most New Yorkers is to look unapproachable, mostly for safety, partly for comfort. Faces on the subway tend to be hidden behind a newspaper or frozen in a serious mask. A smile would indicate vulnerability. It is dehumanizing in many ways. Jesus did not shun the vulnerability that came with His compassion. He didn't politely avert His eyes from obvious human suffering. He was completely there with the person in need. This quality of Christ is so comforting for me. And it is one of the most significant aspects of Jesus that I can give to this city that I love."

"Bloom where you are planted," I've always heard. That doesn't mean "Do the best you can where you've been stuck." It means put down roots, establish friendships, connect with your community. Live, as Julie said, in a state of "heightened awareness." **I am right here, right now, for a purpose.** *Recognize needs. Thrive, don't just take up space. Spread out your leaves, lend beauty and shade, bear fruit. Bloom and release the fragrance. Plant seeds. Live in your neighborhood. Work in your office. Serve on committees. Coach Little League. Cook meals. Fold laundry. Carpool. Ride the subway. Teach English.*

Plant your life.

[1]Blackaby, Henry and Claude King, *Experiencing God* (Nashville: The Sunday School Board, 1990).

[2]Young Life is an interdenominational para-church organization which provides fellowship, evangelism, and discipleship for high school students through local church groups and national summer camps.

3

Revelation

Telling the Truth of God

For this I came into the world, to testify to the truth (John 18:37).

What is God like? What does He think? What is His purpose? "No one has ever seen God," wrote John, "but the only Son...he has explained him" (John 1:18, *my paraphrase*). Jesus spent a large part of His public ministry on earth explaining God. Sometimes, He told a story beginning with, "The kingdom of heaven is like..." At other times, He pointed His finger to say, "The kingdom of heaven is not like..." He also taught by example, through His attitudes and actions. The writer of Hebrews called Jesus the exact representation of God's being (Heb. 1:3). Jesus showed us what God is like—what He thinks, how He acts, what His purpose is.

Isaiah prophesied of Christ, "The people who walk in darkness will see a great light" (Isa. 9:2 NASB). In the Scriptures, darkness usually portrays spiritual blindness; light represents God's truth. "I am the light of the world," Jesus said. "Whoever follows me will never walk in darkness, but will have the light of life"

"You are the light of the world. A city on a hill cannot be hidden. Neither do people light a lamp and put it under a bowl. Instead they put it on its stand, and it gives light to everyone in the house. In the same way, let your light shine before men, that they may see your good deeds and praise your Father in heaven" (Matt. 5:14–16).

(John 8:12). Jesus opened more than just physically blind eyes. He also helped people to see where they had been misled by both their culture and by the church. He corrected wrong thinking about God.

There is a lot of wrong thinking about God out there. Some of it comes from humanism, which tells us we are the center of the universe; we have the power to make things happen. Some of it comes from relativism, the theory that no truth is absolute: what's right for you is right for you, what's right for me is right for me. New Age thought, the occult, horoscopes, psychic networks, crystals...these are truth to many people. Some of our wrong thinking about God comes right out of the pulpit, is broadcast by televangelists, and is published by Christian book companies.

Jesus prayed for us in the Garden of Gethsemane, just before His death. "Sanctify them by the truth; your word is truth" (John 17:17). The word *sanctify* means *to set apart.* The truth of God's Word sets us apart from the world. "In a crooked and perverse generation," Paul wrote to the Philippian believers, "you shine like stars in the universe, as you hold out the word of life" (Phil. 2:15–16).

My pastor, Mike Glenn, said in a sermon: "Long before radar and global-positioned satellites, long before sonar and computer-generated maps, sailors used to find their way by using the stars. They had an instrument called a sextant, and by focusing it on the position of the stars in relation to their position, they could find out where they were and if they were taking the right route. No matter how dark the night or rough the sea, if sailors could find the stars, they could find their way home. In this wonderful passage of Philippians, Paul tells the Christians in Philippi they are the shining stars of the universe." In this swirling, darkened world of wrong thinking, a believer's life firmly fixed on the truth of God is a shining star—a point by which lost and confused people may find their way to the truth.

Rosalie Beck
Rosalie Beck joined the church when she was six to avoid a spanking.

We lived in Hawaii at the time. My father was a career Marine, and my West Texas folks demanded that my brothers and I wear shoes to church. Church was casual at Pali View Baptist Church, especially the evening service, and my friends wore sandals or went barefoot, but not the Beck kids. One night I took my shoes off and sat where my folks couldn't see my feet. (You know how Baptists always sit in the same place for worship!) I reckoned I could scoot out to the car and pretend I had just taken off my shoes. Unfortunately, my folks sat in a different place, and my Dad noticed my bare feet. I knew retribution was awaiting me at home; so, I walked the aisle during the invitation because I knew my folks wouldn't spank a new Christian!

"For twelve years I lived that lie. When I was eighteen, I became a counselor at the San Diego Baptist Association Girls in Action® camp. I had a tent full of fourth grade girls who idolized me. I decided I needed to quit living the lie. Sometime between age 6 and age 18, I had become a Christian; I knew I had to make a formal statement about my walk with God. On the last night of camp, during the invitation, I publicly declared my stand for the Lord."

When did you first understand that this decision would make your life different?

A ctually, my immediate reaction to this realization was terror—that God would make me be a missionary to Africa! Now that I was a public Christian I would have to do God's will, whatever that meant. My assumption was that it would not be pleasant."

God did call Rosalie to missions—not to Africa, but to a different jungle. After attending the University of California at San Diego, she spent two years as a biochemist at the University of Texas Medical School in Houston, Texas. In 1973, through the Journeyman missionary program of the Southern Baptist Convention

(SBC), she served as a youth worker in the cities of Qui Nhon and Dalat, Vietnam. Evacuated in March 1975, Rosalie returned to the United States where she worked with Southeast Asian refugees at the SBC's resettlement office in Fort Smith, Arkansas.

When was the first time you can remember having to choose between being like Christ and being like the culture?

The first conscious decision that I remember making was in junior high. When we chose sides for sports in PE, I always chose a particular girl to be on my team because everyone else rejected her. I was a good athlete and was always team captain. Susan had no athletic ability, but I could see the pain in her face when she was passed over time and again. I always made a point of choosing her early in the selection process. Sometimes the choice meant my team lost, but she felt better about herself and we all had fun anyway. Winning was never that big a deal for me. I like to win; but early on I knew that in Christ, people are far more important than personal achievement or winning."

In January 1976, Rosalie entered Southwestern Baptist Theological Seminary in Fort Worth to work on a Master

"The unfolding of your words gives light; it gives understanding to the simple" (Psalm 119:130).

How has God revealed Himself to you through Scripture?

of Divinity degree. She majored in church history and earned a 4.0 GPA, receiving the first Robert A. Baker Church History Award for the outstanding student in that field. After graduation, Rosalie moved to Waco, Texas, to pursue a Ph.D. in religion at Baylor University. Maintaining a 4.0 GPA in her work, she completed her degree in August 1984. She joined the Baylor faculty in the fall of 1984 and is now an associate professor at the university. Rosalie Beck can claim much personal achievement; but her first priority is still people, and her calling is to make the Word of God come alive to them through her teaching.

When were you first drawn to be a student of the Word?

My parents modeled Bible study for me. I grew up taking part in reading the daily Bible passages and praying out loud during family devotions. Church groups encouraged Bible memorization and study. Because I live so much of my life in my mind, I realized in college that I needed to take seriously the command Jesus gave to love God with my mind as well as my heart (Matt. 22:37). Learning to love God with my mind meant I took time to not just *read* the Bible, but *study* it, believing God would reveal Godself to me through the Scripture. As a church history professor, I have learned that the study of the lives and writings of Christians who have gone before and have been used by God in special ways also deepens my understanding of God."

When did you know you wanted to be a teacher of the Word?

As a journeyman in Vietnam, I taught all the time and loved it. I had never considered teaching as a professional option, but the overseas experience showed me I was a 'natural' for teaching. During my time in Vietnam I often taught Bible studies or led small group discussions of the Bible. At those times I knew that teaching the Bible would always be part of my life. I didn't know in what setting the teaching would take place, but I knew it would. I also knew that I would daily learn more and more.

"Studying Scripture is not a static activity. I learn something new every time I open the text. And I have the obligation before God to use as much outside material as I can to help me understand the Bible. So Hebrew and Greek, archeology, sociology, political science, linguistics—all these areas contribute to my ability to 'correctly handle the word of truth.'" (2 Tim. 2:15).

Tell me about Christ as a teacher.

He was the best! He taught persons, real people who had real needs. He taught them in ways they could

"All Scripture is God–breathed and is useful for teaching, rebuking, correcting and training in righteousness, so that the man of God may be thoroughly equipped for every good work" (2 Tim. 3:16–17).

"But make sure that you don't get so absorbed and exhausted in taking care of all your day–by–day obligations that you lose track of the time and doze off, oblivious to God" (Rom. 13:11, The Message).

What are the day–to–day obligations that absorb you?

understand. His parables were filled with images that the women who listened would understand—leaven in a lump of dough, searching the house for a lost coin. He taught through stories men would understand—a father welcoming home a wayward son, planning for the construction of new barns. He taught *people*—not idealized creatures, but people. He taught at the level of their need. At a time of stress and tension in His life, Jesus took time to teach Mary. She sat at His feet, learning 'the most important things' from God" (Luke 10:38–42).

You know, I realized the implications of that event a few years ago at a very unusual worship service in my church. For several weeks leading up to Easter, our evening services were led by Trent Butler, a member of our church and a respected scholar of the Old Testament. Trent gave us new insight into the privileges believers have because of Christ's sacrifice on the cross. One evening, we experienced how the Jews worshiped before Christ's death. We met in the foyer of the church; only the 'priest' (our pastor) was allowed to enter the sanctuary. The men sat together, reading the Scriptures. The women stood in the back; we were not allowed to have our Bibles.

I saw in that moment what a privilege Christ has given me to sit at His feet and learn. I realize that I am inclined to be a "Martha," too busy to enjoy that privilege. Often the maintenance of my life carries me away, but at heart I think I am a "Mary"; I identify with Jesus most as a teacher. What about you? What quality of Jesus is most significant to you?

Tough question! If I had to choose just one quality, I'd (today) pick Jesus' personal contact with others. Jesus always cared about how His teachings were lived out. He modeled His words by touching lepers, healing the ill, talking to "non-persons" like the woman with the flow of blood, making time to hold children, and noticing how others related to God, like the widow's gift of two mites.

"He lived what He taught. If you look at His life, it illustrates the believer's lifestyle that He Himself described in the Beatitudes (Matt. 5:1–16). Jesus taught His listeners, never underestimating or overestimating their capacity to understand the most important issues in the world. But He always taught persons, not crowds; the farmer, businesswoman, and teenager saw, smelled, heard, and felt as He taught. Jesus put His words into action by really seeing, hearing, knowing the people around Him. The personal element, personal contact, of God with those created in the divine image is incredibly powerful for me."

What quality of Christlikeness is your biggest struggle?

Humility. I'm not using humility as an antonym for pride, either. For me, the humility of Christ meant He accepted people where they were and loved them. He didn't use force to get His ideas across; He allowed people to reject Him and His teachings, He absorbed hurt and pain while continuing to live His life with love, and He knew when not to push His opinion but to let unity and peace prevail. I struggle with that facet of Christ in my life.

"Being Christlike means to take both God and humans seriously; to live a life of love, while remembering the demands of righteousness; to be authentic, real, wherever I am and whatever I do; to spend time apart with God, in prayer and study."

Bible study—especially on our own— is a great mystery to some of us who don't have our Ph.Ds, Rosalie. How do you arrive at the insights you get? What do you do to study?

First, everything is done in an attitude of prayer and willingness to be taught by God, maybe to learn something I never knew or to be confronted with something I had previously ignored.

"When I decide to teach on a passage, I read it over and over, allowing God to show me new things each time. I then look at other passages that talk about the same issues or about persons in the story. For the widow's mite lesson, I looked at everything the Bible teaches about widows and about giving offerings in the temple. After looking at both the Old and New Testaments, I go to my textbooks to learn what I can about the cultural context of the passage. For example, in the widow's story, I checked a book about the role of women in the Judaism of Jesus' day.

"After learning what I can about the context, I look at critical commentaries—commentaries that deal with the language, literary, and cultural issues of the passage. Then I pray, asking God to show me what the Lord wants me and the audience to learn from the passage. What finally crystallizes in my brain may or may not be a major teaching of the text, but it will be a lesson for life with the Lord."

Sounds like a lot of work, doesn't it? That is what Rosalie meant when she said we have a responsibility not to just read the Bible, but study it. That's what it takes to receive a "lesson for life" rather than a thought for the day. Of course, we don't need theology degrees to read the Bible responsibly. At any level of education we can read Scripture with an open mind, ready for the Holy Spirit to teach us.

I met Rosalie when we led a women's conference together in Arkansas. Her insight into the Bible was impressive. She made the three women she talked about that weekend come to life; she made them real. Rosalie herself is authentic, very real. She speaks the truth quietly, with authority.

I wonder, can teaching the truth get you into trouble? Is God's Word controversial?

The answer to both questions is yes! In Romans 12:1 we are told not to conform to the world but to be transformed by 'the renewing of your mind.' In the church, many people don't want to hear the truth of the Bible because God calls on them to change their attitudes and move into the world to make a difference."

Warren Wiersbe, one of my favorite Bible teachers, says, "We only believe as much of the Bible as we practice."[1]

God's Word is always controversial, because it makes demands on us. It calls us to become like Christ, to live lives of love, compassion, mercy, justice, righteousness, and to count everything well lost for the gospel. Those are incredible demands to make on a person. But the effort to study God's Word and to learn from it is well worth time and energy. We are commanded to love God with our minds, not just our hearts. That means study—not just reading, but study."

Is there a difference between knowledge and understanding?

There is a tremendous difference. Knowing something intellectually doesn't mean you understand it. For example, Karla, you knew what the birth process was all about before your first child, but now you understand what it is. I knew about the destructive power of war, but after my time in Vietnam, I understand it.

"For a Christian, knowing something intellectually means you have a certain number of facts that you can arrange and spit out in a given order as needed. But understanding the gospel, understanding what Christ means, goes beyond just facts.

"Sometimes understanding comes with allowing our experience to verify and arrange facts; sometimes understanding comes out of a mental-spiritual link that God grants. Most of us begin to truly understand Christ when we experience Christlikeness in another person."

When we see it lived out. Well, that's what frightens me about "speaking the truth" to the people in my life—because my life has to back it up. And I know it won't always. Rosalie, what do I say when I fail to be Christlike before another person?

Good question. I'm sitting here staring at the keyboard! So many

"For all have
sinned and fall
short of the
glory of God"
(Rom. 3:23).

Where have
you fallen
short? Have
you asked God
to forgive you?
Have you
accepted His
forgiveness and
grace? Have
you admitted
to others your
failure and
God's
faithfulness?

thoughts flit through my mind and heart.

"First, when we fail, we have nothing to say except to God. Asking for forgiveness from the Lord must come first. Then we must forgive ourselves. Then we must ask forgiveness from those we've hurt or wronged by our sin. The confession needs to be only as large as the circle of those who knew they were hurt, no larger."

Acknowledgment of our humanness has to be part of being a disciple. Jesus gave Peter three chances to rectify his denial. Because true Christianity is a lifestyle, anyone who observes a believer in order to truly learn about God will not be "turned off" by one failure to follow God. Lifestyle is the key. If a person confesses Christ, then their overall, through-the-years life will bear that out.

Gloria Gaither

In the fall of 1984, just after my first son was born, I boarded a bus to travel as a background singer for the Bill Gaither Trio. For more than three decades, Bill and Gloria Gaither have been in the ministry of "revelation." Their songs, books, and most recently their video series have given us glimpses into the kingdom. In the years that I traveled with them, I saw the convictions and the insights expressed in those words and music lived out before me.

Gloria Gaither has spent most of her life helping people to recognize "the things that last forever." In doing so, she has talked a lot about her family—not only her three children (and grandchildren), but the parents who tremendously shaped her own view of the kingdom. For Gloria, salvation came at an exceptionally young age.

I remember that you prayed to accept Christ during a family prayertime.

We had family worship. My Dad (who was a pastor) would read the Scripture and we would all share prayer requests. Some of them were pretty heavy, and often my Dad would have one of us pray about some major phone call that came in or something that happened at church. And so it never occurred to me that it was an 'us' or 'them' thing. I was included, even as a child. That is actually what brought me to Christ.

"I was four years old and had gotten to the stage where my sister, who was older than I, would be left in charge of me. I remember getting really mad at my sister. I mean, I was so angry, that I experienced hatred for the first time. I ran outside and threw myself down in the grass.

"In the grass was a granddaddy-long-legs spider. My mother had taught us never to kill these helpless creatures; we were not allowed to harm any life.

When we found them in the house, she'd always make us carry them outside. So here in the grass was this granddaddy-long-legs, and I picked him up and pulled off one of his legs! I'd just watch his little body shiver and pulsate, and then I'd pull off another leg. I kept on torturing this tiny creature until he was nothing but a little bubble of a body; and I put him back in the grass, turned my back on him and walked away.

"Oh, did I feel guilty! First, because I had violated nature—and not even just killed the creature. (I was always taught that if something was badly injured you needed to kill it quickly and not let it suffer). Second, because I knew that what I had done to the spider, I had really done to my sister in my heart. That day it was as if everything had died in me. But my parents treated me the same—they treated me like a Christian, a responsible part of our ministering family. The day spun its way toward our worship time and I dreaded it. I knew that there would be prayer requests and I would be considered capable of praying for them. It was this being treated as a Christian that really convicted me.

"My Dad began to pray, and I was just overwhelmed with guilt and began to cry. I remember crawling across the floor to my Mother and whispering, 'I need to pray.' And she took me seriously. Without even missing a beat, she touched my Dad on the arm in the middle of his prayer and said, 'Gloria needs to pray.' Neither one of them said, 'She just did,' or 'She's too little.' They just said, 'What is it, Gloria?'

"I told them what I had done and that I needed forgiveness. I felt everything that I have since heard people describe as being a part of the conversion experience. It felt like a brick wall had been lifted off my neck. I felt like I could fly! I felt an overwhelming sense of compassion, and I probably prayed the longest prayer on record for a four-year-old! I prayed for all the missionaries, all the people at church who weren't saved, my grandpa who rolled his own cigarettes out behind the barn ...you know, that whole amazing love for people that comes from receiving the love of Jesus. I remember when I went to bed, I couldn't wait to get up because I thought, 'Tomorrow, I'm going to act different.'

"Well, I got up the next morning and I felt like a lump! I remember coming downstairs into the kitchen where my Mother was cooking breakfast. She turned around—I must've been just standing there *looking* like a lump—and she said, 'What's the matter?'

"I said, 'I don't feel like I did last night. I just felt so free and new and wonderful last night, and I don't feel that now.'

"She said, 'Have you done anything since last night?' and I said, 'No.'

"She said, 'Has God pointed out anything specific that you might need to

"While Jesus was having dinner at Matthew's house, many tax collectors and 'sinners' came and ate with him and his disciples. When the Pharisees saw this, they asked his disciples, 'Why does your teacher eat with tax collectors and "sinners"?' On hearing this, Jesus said, 'It is not the healthy who need a doctor, but the sick. But go and learn what this means: "I desire mercy, not sacrifice." For I have not come to call the righteous, but sinners.'" (Matt. 9:10–13).

Who are the "tax collectors" around you?

pray about?' and I said 'No.'

"Then my mother knelt beside me, on my eye level. 'Well, that's your first lesson in being a Christian: Don't go by feelings, go by faith. God said He would accept you, and it is by grace you have a new life. When God convicts you that there's something wrong, He doesn't play games. He'll tell you exactly what it is and what you should do about it.' And she said, 'If you have that gray feeling, like a fog, that's Satan trying to confuse you. You need to simply pray, rebuke the devil, and go about your business.'"

Do you think that attitude—including you as if you could understand—would work with adults and friends, people who aren't Christians?

You know, I've found it to be more effective than preaching at them. I just talk about the Lord, and I try not to use ecclesiastical terms—our little church buzz words and our particular denominational terms, whether it's 'anointed' or 'assured' or 'justified.' They don't understand all that."

And they don't need to! I was preparing to teach a Bible study on the Samaritan woman, and I realized that she was the first person in John's account to whom Jesus ever said, "I am the one" (John 4:26). She wasn't the kind of person that I might have chosen for a theological discussion.

I think God, of course, did that on purpose. First, she was a woman. She was a harlot; she was unacceptable. She was not in with the religious 'insiders' as far as her race and religious affiliation. She was, in fact, an outcast in her own community. And maybe that's why He could say it to her—because she was full of questions and not so full of answers."

Jesus reveals Himself to seekers—people with more questions than answers. And seekers come in all shapes and sizes. Sometimes they look like astrologers from the East. Sometimes they look like shepherds. Sometimes they look like Nicodemus, a religious man. Sometimes they look like lepers. And sometimes they do look like a rebellious teenager or an ambitious yuppie. All around us—every day—are seekers. They may not know it is God they're looking for, but He is pursuing them. And He doesn't wait for them to become "religious" or "acceptable" before He reveals Himself.

The thing that is most amazing to me is that Jesus was regular. He laid down His Godness—and the temptation in the wilderness was all about Satan trying to get Jesus to use His Godness in every way, in every area of life for earthly reasons. So when Scripture says that He did not consider Himself to be

"My message and my preaching were not with wise and persuasive words, but with a demonstration of the Spirit's power, so that you faith might not rest on men's wisdom, but on God's power." (1 Cor. 2:4–5).

Do any people tend to put you on a pedestal? How can you make sure that God, not you, gets the credit?

God, but took upon Himself the form of a servant, I don't think that meant that He did "servant" kinds of things for people. We don't have any record of Him carrying in somebody's groceries or helping old people across the street; that's what we tend to think when we read that. I think what it means is that the most lowly servant, the most uneducated person, or the greatest person felt like Jesus was one of them. He spent 30 years of His life just being one of them.

"And when He talked to the farmer, He said, 'I'll tell you a story: a farmer went out to sow some seeds.' When He talked to the fishermen, He said, 'Cast out and get a fish. Cut it open; here's a coin,' or 'I will make you fishers of men.' He did not play God to them. He didn't act God-ish. And that is the amazing thing, that is the miraculous thing: that this God chose to put Himself in such limits—self-imposed limits—that He was one of us, and it was never condescending.

"That quality of Christ is probably the most significant thing I deal with every day I live: to disassemble any kind of pedestal that people put you on because you know that that is not of God. To say, 'How can I be regular?' I *am* regular. I know that about myself: I am regular. I stick my foot in my mouth, and I wash my clothes just like everybody else. And so any pretense to be anything other than regular has to be consciously disassembled."

Why? Because otherwise people don't see a Christ they can relate to, a Christ Who would accept them? Because they have problems, and apparently you don't.

Exactly. And the tendency, I think, is to prove that we are indeed Christ-like by hiding any of our flaws. ('Well, if I really were a Christian I wouldn't still be doing this, would I? So let's not let anybody know I do.') I don't agree with applauding our own faults; we are constantly at work on ourselves. The struggle for me on an ongoing basis is that paradox, the constant everyday working paradox that you don't *earn* salvation, but you are never at rest at working on stuff that God points out in your life. The incredible paradox of Christ is that salvation, on the one hand, produces some results in our behavior; and yet, on the other hand, no matter what we do, we could never earn it. And that's the struggle: to live that paradox."

So what many of us do is we busy ourselves with a kind of Christian version of self-improvement. A checklist.

Yes, and we consider that holiness. But holiness...I think people who are becoming Christlike have no idea what God is up to in them. I think most of the people that I consider Christlike consider themselves failures in that area. It's only other people that can see that you are being shaped into the image of

"He who belongs to God hears what God says. The reason you do not hear is that you do not belong to God" (John 8:47; 10:26–27).

Is there some area of your life in which you do not hear God? What barriers have you put up between you and Him?

"He has also set eternity in the hearts of men" (Ecc. 3:11).

God has placed within you a sense of what's eternal. Consider the things you think are keeping you from serving God. Could these be the very things He can use to do eternal things? Can you see how this could matter eternally?

Christ. You can't see it yourself, and if you start to see it in yourself, it's probably not real. I think the quality that serving Christ begins to bring out in you is an incredible humility—a feeling that you are never getting there. The closer you get to God, the more clearly you can see how inadequate you are in comparison to him.

"Maybe to be Christlike is to be in process. What we consider the process, God considers the goal. The goal is relationship. Any circumstance of life that crowds us to Christ is what He's after. What we consider process is making us more intimate with Him, and intimacy with Him is what He's after."

The stuff that we think is getting in our way—the kids, the bills, this problem with my mother, this job—that's not keeping us from knowing Him. That's where He can show Himself to us—and where He can show Himself to others through us.

I meet people who say, 'I could be a great servant of the Lord with my talents if I weren't limited by caring for this invalid, or this child, or this job.' How ironic! We're going to get to the end of life, and God's not going to say, 'How many words did you publish?' He's going to say, 'What did you *become?*' And how our daily life is lived out with one other human being who is an eternal soul may be far more important than what we get done by the world's accounting. I could've said, 'If I didn't have my little kids to raise....' Well, here are three kids that are eternal souls. I *know* that's eternal business. The rest of the stuff I've done, I don't know, but that I know is eternal. There is no doubt about it.

"My daughter just walked in, and I look at her and I say, 'Boy, mothering her was a good choice.' I watch her mothering her child and teaching him eternal concepts, and I see her affecting the world—writing and communicating and multiplying myself a thousand times on into a generation that I will not live to see. I know that's eternal. And what book would have been worth that?"

I don't think Gloria is advocating that I must stay at home with my kids or else I can't teach them eternal things, because she was a working mother. But I was challenged by her that what I accomplish is not as important as whether the people around me understand that Christ is my motivation for accomplishing those things.

How did you teach your kids about the things that last forever?

I felt when I was raising our children that they didn't become holy by 'cocooning.' I don't think that protecting them from exposure to things necessarily would make them virtuous. I don't think innocence is the same thing as virtue; innocence is what happens before you have any exposure to evil. It's what Adam and Eve were when they were first created. Virtue was what they could have chosen after the Fall. And the Fall happens to us all; it's a fact of life for all of us and our children. I think we should protect our children's innocence and not allow our children to be robbed of their childhoods by over-exposing them to evil. But having said that, I don't think we can make them Christians by cocooning them either.

"When we were raising our children we wanted to help them learn to deal with whatever they were going to come in contact with while we had them, so that together we could say, 'What does the Bible say about this? How do we deal with this? What about this person? What about this lie?'

"I also believe that when we cocoon them, we rob our children of the chance to understand what missions is all about. We had a lot of children in and out of our home from broken homes, kids who had siblings who were drug-addicted…and amazingly most of those children were way better than they ought to have been, based on the influences they had. Our children grew up with a sense that they could impact another person's life, that they were responsible to do that—that Christianity was a chosen behavior, not something that came because they had never been exposed to anything else."

"One of the biggest sins, according to Jesus Christ, is self-righteousness. And I think that often the children of Christian homes grow up hearing it's the good 'us' against the big bad 'they.'

Well, I'm afraid that the "theys" will be a big influence on my kids.

Why not *your* kids be a big influence on *them?* That comes by gradually building moral muscle; it doesn't come by keeping them away from anything evil. Christ came to teach us how to be *in* the world and not *of* it. We are a lot better at being *of* the world but not *in* it.

"As parents we can't cover all the "whats" our children will face with rules. We're preparing them to live in a world that does not yet exist. We can't teach our kids *what* to think; we must teach them *how* to think. We often believe that if we insulate them and teach them *what* to think, and there are no influences that challenge them as they grow up, we've made them Christian. But the truth is, you know, we'd better equip them to think, to believe— and then gradually give them a chance to try their wings while we still have them. In this process of learning and growing, they're going to make some mistakes. We're still making a few!"

I'm still making many. It took me years to admit that. For a long time, I

"For who has known the mind of the Lord, that he may instruct him? But we have the mind of Christ" (1 Cor. 2:16).

In which areas do you need to think more with the mind of Christ?

tried to pretend that I understood it all and had it mastered. I don't know who I thought I was fooling; certainly not the people who knew me. Only recently I have learned to say, "I'm having trouble with this part." Jeannette Clift George helped me to see that. Jeannette has a delightful way of expounding some great and deep truths from God's word, which she follows by her delightful laugh that says, "Can you believe I missed that point?"

Jeannette Clift George

My first glimpse of Jeannette Clift George was her role as Corrie Ten Boom in the film *The Hiding Place*, the story of a Dutch woman who saved the lives of countless Jews during the Nazi occupation. Her acting credits also include off-Broadway and touring productions with the New York Shakespeare Company. Founder and artistic director of the A.D. Players, a Houston-based Christian theater company now in its 31st season, Jeannette is an author, speaker, and a leader in the professional development of the Christian arts. She told me about the early steps in her spiritual journey.

I made a decision for Christ when I was a little girl. But at a point in my life I began to wander away from the home-cooked faith and dismiss as meaningless the form of faith my parents expressed.

It wasn't so much a disbelief in God as a denial of Him in the agenda of life. I thank God that I didn't get lost in that confusion."

What brought you back?

A friend gave me a copy of the Phillips Translation of the New Testament, and I began reading it. Literally from the pages of the Bible I reckoned with the love of God and the relationship He offered me, and that personal identity rests in no other source but God. So, in an apartment in New York City where I was working in theater, I turned my life over to Christ as Savior and Lord. Each day since that day I have had a deeper understanding of what the Lordship of Christ means...and what it doesn't mean.

"It doesn't mean that my hair will become naturally curly, or that everybody will love me, or that troubles will never touch me, or that pecan pie will no longer be calorie heavy! It *does* mean that I can trust God, that He will never assign me to do what He has not equipped me to do, that He will never desert me in my search for His will, and that He will bring from me the potential He has given me.

"I am a very emotional person. I have my ups and downs and ins and outs. But one of the most comforting facts about Christ is not only that He Himself is the Comforter, but that He is sovereign and bigger than my ups and

downs, ins and outs. God is involved in
my life, even in my disposition—that
quality of Christ refreshes me with each
recall of its truth. Jesus—with us. I
guess that is most significant to me: God
Almighty is intimately involved in the
life of Jeannette.

*Jesus has to keep reminding me of
that. I tend to keep Him in a box. Sometimes knowingly, but usually without
realizing it, I do what you said: I deny
Him in the agenda of life. I think we
tend to label parts of our lives as Christian or secular—to say, 'This is my work,
this is my faith.*

I must admit that my work doesn't have
to be Christian in order to reveal God.
God will reveal Himself in anything He
chooses to use.

"He can be equally evident in disobedience and in obedience, because He is
the sovereign God. But the disobedient
miss the joy of participation. Because
God loves us, He uses us.

"Frequently the only believer in a
company of theater people, I knew a
kind of spiritual loneliness in the practice of my craft, but generally found a
warm fellowship within the bonding of
the craft. Theater people are religious
by nature and drawn to mystical formats
and practices. They often have a very
limited view of true Christianity.
The world of secular theater is a world
of deep religious content. We need to
recognize that. Christian theater is not
unusual because it worships, it is
unusual because of *Whom* it worships.

Christian theater is theater that has been given back to the One Who gave the gift in the first place and thus it becomes Christian service."

The arts can be the very instrument of God's contemporary revelation of Himself. The Christian artist is simply revealing the nature and relevance of God. The purpose of the arts is a unique communication: God to man, man to man, man to God. Even the classical Greek writers struggling with their myths and legends were creating tapestries of relationship between their fabled gods and man. I hope the contemporary church is catching on to the potential of the arts, not only for communicating the gospel, but applying it to our worldview, to the disciplines of life, to our place in society, to our rights to feelings."

What would you say to a young Christian who wants to be involved in the arts? Would you steer her toward Christian arts, or would you advise her how to reveal Christ in secular theater?

Christian theater is far more difficult than secular theater, but the believer in Christian theater must come to grips with the fact that the chances he or she will ever become a star are very slim."

That's the rub in the arts, isn't it—the clash of mission against ego. Come to think of it, that's the rub for all of us, artist or accountant!

"Whatever you do, work at it with all your heart, as working for the Lord, not for men, since you know that you will receive an inheritance from the Lord as a reward. It is the Lord Christ you are serving" (Col. 3:23–24).

"For it is not the one who commends himself who is approved, but the one whom the Lord commends" (2 Cor. 10:18).

Do you need to receive recognition or agreement from others in order to feel your service is validated?

I think true Christlikeness is in secure identity. Christ had no second agenda to prove in order to know Himself to be Who He was. The truly Christlike person wastes no energy in trying to establish identity through recognition or even agreement. She knows *Whose* she is and therefore *who* she is, and she reaches out to meet the needs of others under the assignment of God. I love 1 Corinthians 9:16, in which Paul says, 'I am compelled to preach the Gospel.'

Paul goes on in that verse to say, 'Woe is me if I don't!' We would like to choose which moments to be vessels of Christ's revelation of Himself to the world, to somehow control the flow of His Spirit through us. Paul had yielded that control. In all situations—prison or pulpit— he did not—could not—stem the flow. He did not separate his life into piles, like laundry; all of life was an opportunity to let Christ be seen. He did not get paid for it; he did not wait for someone to appoint him a position in which to speak the truth. God had appointed him to do it. It was Paul's purpose in life, much like Jesus, who said, 'Let us go somewhere else…so I can preach there also. That is why I have come' (Mark 1:38). Jesus did not need the title Messiah; He did not need the Pharisee's blessing or the popularity of the crowds to speak the truth. It was His purpose.

It is yours, too. It's not the preacher's

job. You don't have to be a Sunday school teacher or wait for an outreach event to speak the truth of the gospel in your workplace, your backyard, at the mall, over dinner. As Paul said, it is "something solemnly entrusted to you."[2] You have already been appointed to "go and preach" (Matt. 28:19–20).

"But you also must testify," Jesus said, "for you have been with me from the beginning" (John 15:27).

[1]Wiersbe, Warren W. *The Bible Exposition Commentary*, (Wheaton: Victor Books, 1989), vol.2, 352.
[2]Peterson, Eugene, *The Message* (Colorado Springs: NavPress, 1994), 35.

4

Compassion

Demonstrating the Nature of God

*When he saw the crowds, he had com-
passion on them, because they were
harassed and helpless, like sheep without
a shepherd* (Matt. 9:36).

If you've ever witnessed the behavior of
sheep, you know that sheep are stupid.
They really are. Ask any sheep farmer.
When Jesus said, "I am the good shepherd" (John 10:14*a*). He was talking to
people who understood firsthand what
sheep are like. They are dirty, and they
are dumb. They have no sense of direction and are easily distracted, wandering
off from the flock and getting themselves into all kinds of trouble. And they
are completely incapable of getting
themselves out of it.

Jesus looked at the crowds who followed Him, and He saw the same traits.
And He was moved to compassion. He
was moved to heal them, feed them,
raise their dead—but not because that
would fix them. It wouldn't. Jesus
reached out to the helpless in compassion so they might know the Shepherd.
He showed them the nature of God.

When John the Baptist heard of Jesus'

ministry, he sent his own disciples to ask, "Are you the one we've been waiting for?" John had said that the kingdom of heaven was close at hand. In effect, he was asking, "Is this it?"

"Jesus replied, 'Go back and report to John what you hear and see: The blind receive sight, the lame walk, those who have leprosy are cured, the deaf hear, the dead are raised, and the good news is preached to the poor" (Matt. 11:2–5). In the kingdom of heaven, there will be no more tears, no diseases, no sadness, no lack (Rev. 21:1–4). That is the way God meant it to be. Our poverty, spiritual and material, is a result of our wandering, like lost sheep, into places He never intended us to go.

God's nature is to comfort, to provide. One day we will all know Him fully. Until then, Jesus said, here's a preview.

Rosalynn Carter

Former First Lady Rosalynn Carter has worked for more than two decades to improve the quality of life for people around the world. Today, she is an advocate for mental health, early childhood immunization, human rights conflict resolution, and the empowerment of urban communities through her work at The Carter Center in Atlanta, Georgia (a private, nonprofit institution founded by former President and Mrs. Carter in 1982). She is the author of *First Lady From Plains, Everything Thing to Gain: Making the Most of the Rest of Your Life*

(co-written with Jimmy Carter) and
*Helping Yourself Help Others: A Book for
Caregivers* (co-written with Susan K.
Golant).

Rosalynn Smith Carter was born in
Plains, Georgia, where she met and
married Jimmy Carter. From the heritage
of their faith, they have reached out in
compassion to people around the world,
not only through their public service in
government, but as volunteers in projects like Habitat for Humanity.

In her autobiography *First Lady of
Plains*, Rosalynn tells of her Christian
upbringing.

We had no movie theater, no
library, no recreation center, in
Plains. Occasionally someone would
open a restaurant, but it would never
last very long. The social life of the
community revolved around the
churches. My grandmother Murray was
Lutheran, my grandfather Baptist, and
my parents Methodist. I went to all
three churches—almost every time the
doors opened, it seemed—to Sunday
school and regular church services, to
prayer meeting, Methodist League, Baptist Girls' Auxiliary, and Bible school.

"God was a real presence in my life.
We were taught to love Him and felt
very much the necessity and desire to
live the kind of life He would have us
live, to love one another and be kind to
and help those who needed help."[1]

*In the seventh grade, through the
influence of a teacher, young Rosalynn
Smith began to realize that the boundaries of the world extended beyond
Plains, Georgia.*

She further explains in her book.

One day Miss MacArthur brought a
map of the world to school and
told us that there was a war in Europe
and that it was important we know
about it. Each day she assigned a different student the task of bringing the class
up-to-date on the war news. For the first
time in my life, I began searching news-
papers to discover a world of interesting
people and faraway places, but also a
menacing and ominous world. I worried
about all the terrible things that were
happening as war approached, and lay
in bed at night, hoping it would go
away somehow. The year was 1939,
however, and that was not to happen."[2]

*Her concern for the world found
expression when as First Lady she
became an advocate and advisor on
mental health and caregiving issues.*

My work in mental health has taught
me how important it is for people

of faith to help people who are disadvantaged and to support their needs to our social and governmental institutions. Members of churches and other faith groups can be advocates for those who cannot speak for themselves.

"People of faith can work not only to help individuals, but to help whole communities. Congregations can make a big difference simply by organizing respite care for those tending to chronically ill family members. These projects are often not technically difficult. Almost anyone in a congregation can stay for awhile with someone who is ill to give the caregiver some time off or help with transportation or grocery shopping."

I can think of several people I know who could use my help in this way: a neighbor who is a single, working mother of four; a friend who cares for a daughter with disabilities; my mom, who is the one responsible for any care or assistance my grandmother needs. I can start there. But how would my church know about people in our community who need this help?

Sometimes there is a gap between the traditional commitments of faith groups to public service and the day-to-day practices, because congregations don't always have models of service programs that can be implemented. At The Carter Center in Atlanta, we have an Interfaith Health Program that has identified hundreds of models of

"If anyone has material possessions and sees his brother in need but has no pity on him, how can the love of God be in him? Dear children, let us not love with words or tongue but with actions and in truth" (1 John 3:17–18).

What specific actions have you taken to help someone in need in your community?

effective health ministries. And at the Rosalynn Carter Institute of Georgia Southwestern State University, we provide information on caregiving to congregations and other organizations or individuals willing to donate their time."

In the book Helping Yourself Help Others, *Rosalynn further explains how important it is for churches to be involved in caring for the community.*

As part of a CARE-NET study [at the Institute], we asked whether the family caregivers in our area looked to their religious institutions to alleviate some of their isolation and their burden. This is, after all, southwest Georgia, the heart of the "Bible Belt," and we anticipated that many would find solace in their church.

"Some of the responses we received were startling at the very least. As expected, 86 percent of the informal caregivers said that their religious beliefs were very important to their lives. Seventy percent said that their church provided them spiritual guidance that helped them with the caregiving. During the interviews, family caregivers often disclosed that they turned to prayer and belief in God as their source of strength.

"But when we asked family caregivers how much concrete support (such as money, respite, transportation, or supplies) they received from their religious institutions, only 10 percent replied that they received help! And more than two-thirds of our participants said that their church was providing inadequate assistance.

"I suppose I shouldn't have been so surprised by this. When I was teaching Sunday school before Jimmy became governor, every year my class would put together a basket of food and canned goods for a needy family. But we didn't know who to give it to. We had to go to the welfare department to find an impoverished family. The church couldn't tell us which families in our community needed help.

"When a member falls ill, we all pray for him or her and the minister goes to the hospital or home to visit, but I think religious institutions should take a more active role in informing people about health issues and in helping with some of the caregivers' practical problems, including transportation and respite.[3]

"Religion has been a big part of my life. So has politics. The problems I have seen, the ones that reach the governor's desk or the president's desk, are the ones that don't go away. But government can never solve all the problems."

Having reached the pinnacle of achievement in public service, Jimmy and Rosalynn Carter left the White House in 1980, returning to their home in Plains, Georgia, their family business

"Religion that God our Father accepts as pure and faultless is this: to look after orphans and widows in their distress and to keep oneself from being polluted by the world" (James 1:27).

Notice: it's equally important to God that we look out for the helpless as it is that we look out for our own condition.

"For I know the plans I have for you," declares the Lord, "plans to prosper you and not to harm you, plans to give you hope and a future" (Jer. 29:11).

Are you at a turning point— a "change of seasons"? Have you asked God what His plan is for you?

in bankruptcy. Before them stretched the second half of their lives. What would they do with it?

"There is a time for everything," the writer of Ecclesiastes said. (Eccl. 3:1a). There are seasons in our lives when we think we have more to offer God than others. The important thing to remember is that there is never a time when God cannot use us. Although the time comes when our duties as parent, caregiver, employee, manager, or president are done, we are never retired from God's service. At the moment the world is done with us, we may be just on the brink of our greatest usefulness to God.

In the book Everything to Gain: Making the Most of the Rest of Your Life *coauthored by Jimmy and Rosalynn, Rosalynn tells how together they are learning to use their talents for God in every stage of life.*

In a recent Sunday school discussion, we talked about what we might do that would enable us to experience a sense of joy and peace in times of adversity. There was general agreement that we should inventory our talents and interests, that our goals in life should be worthy as measured by God, that we should attempt things that might be beyond our abilities, and that this would put us in a spirit of submission to God's will. Once we do all this, we can then undertake worthy goals with boldness and confidence, realizing that these revised ambitions might be quite different from the more self-serving achievements we had previously coveted."[4]

One of those worthy goals the Carters have undertaken has been their work as volunteers and advocates for Habitat for Humanity. Founded by Millard Fuller, Habitat for Humanity builds low-cost housing for families around the world. Homeowners are required to participate with a "sweat equity," working alongside a cross-section of volunteers, from college students to retirees. Following biblical principles, the homes are financed by Habitat at zero percent interest.

The Carters' first experience with Habitat was to organize and participate in a volunteer team from their community, renovating a dilapidated building in the lower east side of New York City.

I was first assigned, along with two other women, to clean up the floor that still remained in one corner of the back section. We scraped up layers of old glue and paint and patches of linoleum that were stuck to it, removed nails that were sticking up, and had made it perfectly smooth, when one of the men came over with a sheet of plywood and said, 'Nail it down.' Nail it down? Before we left home I had told Jimmy that I would do anything but hammer. At first it took me fifteen or twenty strokes for each nail, but before

"Rich and poor
have this in
common: The
Lord is the
Maker of them
all" (Prov.
22:2).

the week was over I could drive one in
with only four or five strokes!

"The next day Jimmy made me fore-
man of the back half of the second
floor, which would eventually be two
apartments. And with three other
women and an occasional male volunteer, before the week was over we had
laid the subfloor and the floor in our
entire section. The last day when we
were racing against the clock to get our
section finished, we had one piece of
flooring left to put in place. It was in an
awkward spot that fit around a brick
chimney and tapered off at one end. We
measured it, sawed the wood, held our
breath, and dropped it in place. It was
perfect! A perfect fit! We screamed, 'We
did it! We did it!'

"Jimmy came running from the front
of the building: 'What's the matter?
Who's hurt?' When he saw what we had
done, even he was impressed—and we
all signed our names to that one piece
of flooring on the second floor in a new
apartment in a New York City slum."⁵

*So now a family is walking around on
a floor that bears the signature of the
former President and First Lady of the
United States! But coming to terms with
new experiences in life hasn't always
come easy for Rosalynn. When Jimmy lost
the re-election to the presidency, she
struggled to see the hand of God.*

I don't understand it. I just don't understand why God wanted us to lose the election,' I would say. Jimmy was always more mature in his Christian attitude than I was. He would say, 'It's hard for us to accept the fact that our priorities are not the same as God's. We attach too much importance to things like popularity, wealth and political success. To Him problems that often seem most important to us at the time are really not very significant. But God trusts us to make the best use of the time we have, to try to live like Jesus and to make our lives meaningful to others no matter where we are.'"[6]

Rosalynn Carter had a picture of her life, her future. You and I do too. But her picture was shattered. In picking up the pieces, she found that God had a very different vision.

God uses broken people, whose image of themselves has been shattered, to extend His compassion to other broken people.

Peggy Overbey

Peggy Overbey has experienced God's compassion, and today God is using Peggy to demonstrate His compassion to others.

"Do not say, 'Why were the old days better than these?' For it is not wise to ask such a question. As you do not know the path of the wind, or how the body is formed in a mother's womb, so you cannot understand the work of God, the Maker of all things" (Eccl. 7:10; 11:5).

"So from now on we regard no one from a worldly point of view" (2 Cor. 5:16).

The world does not measure people's value in the same way God does. Check your eyesight: which point of view do you share?

There are two Scripture verses, Philippians 2:3 and Romans 12:10, that say the same thing: 'Honor one another above yourselves.' When you walk in a place where you learn that your total sufficiency has to be on the Lord Jesus Christ and not anything that you've done, when you can say with David in Psalm 118:17, 'I will not die but live, and will proclaim what the Lord has done. The Lord has chastened me severely, but he has not given me over to death,' then it puts a different outlook on what people need. That's why I love people.

"You have to have an understanding that you have no strength of your own, no power without Christ. When you understand that for yourself, you can't help but have compassion on others who are hurting or needy. You can treat them with honor—even people who are not in honorable circumstances.

"My sister has a memory of the time a little girl came to our church in North Carolina, and because she didn't have clothes I made her a dress on Sunday afternoon. I have no memory of that! But through the years I've always cared about people's needs—whether they were physical, or just needed a friend, or whatever. I haven't always been able to do as much until probably the last 20 years."

There are a lot of people in the world meeting needs, Peggy—Peace Corps

workers, social workers, community programs. We can give people a bag of groceries, we can give them clothes to wear,
but you know and I know that's not
going to change their lives, that's not
going to give them the power to turn
around. How do you know when it's
time to go beyond?

Beyond just meeting a physical or
material need? Start at the beginning. I start with Christ and meeting the
material/physical need. I don't think
there's any other way to start. I can give
somebody food first, but at the same
time I will say, 'God is the One Who
will supply all of your needs.' I don't
think that I need to give them food this
week and then wait until they come
back next time to tell them where the
source of real food comes from."

*That's true. In her work with the
benevolence ministry of her church and
with GraceWorks, a joint endeavor with
other churches in the area, Peggy has
always made it clear what real needs
are. She is willing to look a person in the
eye and say, "Let's find you a job and a
place to live, but that's not going to do
you much good if you don't know Jesus."*

*I mean, Peggy, you are just downright
fearless!*

"I tell you the truth, whatever you did for one of the least of these brothers of mine, you did for me" (Matt. 25:40).

Working with benevolence ministry has given me an outlet, but if I were not on the committee, I would do the same thing. It's just what I do. I don't go anywhere where it doesn't exist. Part of that is because God increases our awareness when we are willing to say to Him, 'Use me in this area.'

"For example, last year I was at a Christian conference in a huge convention center. I went down to get a cup of coffee and a doughnut, and I guess there were about 500 people eating food. I saw this homeless man standing over by a corner. Now you ask me, how did I know he was homeless? I didn't know, but I could tell he didn't fit in with the rest of the people—and one real good giveaway is that he was looking in the garbage cans! And no one approached the man, out of 6,000 people at this Christian conference.

"So I went over and said, 'Could I buy you some coffee and a doughnut?' He said, 'That would be nice,' and I said, 'Well, come on and get in line with me.'

"He said, 'No, I can't do that!' and I said, 'I'll be glad to buy you something; just come on and get in line.' But he was afraid of being thrown out by the security guards for panhandling.

"I got back up to the auditorium and said to my friend, 'I can't believe nobody was going to help that man.' To me that's inconceivable. I can't imagine that no one saw him!"

*They might have seen him, Peggy; but
I would have been afraid to say something, that I would say the wrong thing.
I don't know what we're afraid of. Why
on earth would I think someone that
needy would reject my offer to help?*

Sometimes poor people aren't nice to
you, because they feel that you have
more than they have. And their language is not always good; their attitude
is not good. Which in turn makes you
have to get rough with the things you
say or do, too. I always say I didn't
even know how to cuss until I started
working with benevolence! I've got a
long list now!"

*Peggy laughs that devilishly earthy
laugh that shows in her life, there is no
"us" and "them." (Peggy Overbey always
looks like she has just gotten away with
something she shouldn't have!) Then, she
grows serious, speaking frankly.*

You *are* outside your comfort zone.
The only way that you ever find
people that need Jesus Christ and/or
food and clothing is to live in the world,
not of the world. Most of the people
that I associate with are not our ordinary Christian ladies and friends. I have
Christian friends, and I love to do things
with them; but the truth is, Karla, if I
had to choose between you or somebody that I thought needed a lunch

"And who knows but that you have come to royal position for such a time as this?" (Esther 4:14).

Consider what stage of life or position you have come to. What could God do through you now that He could not at another time in your life?

more than you need a lunch, I would have to choose that other person. I've never been afraid to ask them to my home."

Now that's way outside my comfort zone! Even when you had children at home?

Well, I didn't deal with the same kind of people when I had children. And that makes a big difference."

So, to some extent, it's your availability.

Right. There's a difference between having a generous heart (and being able to teach your children to have a generous heart) and always dragging home everybody you see. I'm firmly convinced that God does not put into our path that which He has not equipped us to do at a certain time in our life. I don't think there's any way that He's going to say to you at your stage of life the things He's saying to me now—like coming home and finding a fellow I'm working with, an armed robber, with a .22 caliber gun and five joints of marijuana that he wants to leave at my house. But God didn't ask that of me when I had small children. And I think that part of the guilt and the frustration we've assumed comes from trying to do everything that needs to be done, rather than that which God has put at hand—which for you is your family.

"Another thing that makes a difference in availability is money. I couldn't have bought somebody a Bible, or whatever, when my kids were little. See, I feel God has called me to be accountable now, with the resources that I have now. I have more resources, and I'd rather use them for somebody else than to buy myself something.

And that's an evidence that Christ lives in you, because the human thing to do is to look out for yourself. It requires God's love—the kind of love that would lay down His Son's life—to naturally want to put someone else's comfort above ours. That's God-nature, not human-nature.

I have to be dead honest: I question 'Lord, do I do this because I want people to say *Oh, you do such a good job*, or do I do this because You told me to?' Do you ever question that?"

Absolutely. I suspect that a lot of the "good works" that are done in and through our churches are done to make us feel better about ourselves.

People say, 'Don't you want to see some results?' I don't know anybody that doesn't, but that's not the reason that I do what I do. I do what I do because Jesus said, 'You're to live this way; you're to look out for others' needs before your own needs.' He healed ten lepers; only one thanked Him.

"You can't be their savior. You can

"So when you give to the needy, do not announce it with trumpets, as the hypocrites do in the synagogues and on the streets, to be honored by men..." (Matt. 6:2–4).

help them, but at some point they have to take responsibility for their lives. You can equip them and share the Lord with them so they can do that."

T.J. Williams

Equipping women to build a new life and introducing them to the One Who can give them new life is the work of Christian Women's Job Corps™ (CWJC). A ministry of Woman's Missionary Union® (WMU), Auxiliary to the Southern Baptist Convention, CWJC provides a Christian context in which impoverished women can be equipped for life and employment. During their course of training, each client is matched with a mentor who encourages them, prays with them, and provides assistance. CWJC has been recognized by the White House as a viable program for assisting women in the transition from welfare to work. T.J. Williams is the Business Administrator of the CWJC site in San Antonio, Texas, one of the first pilot projects begun in January 1996.

T.J. was eight when she became a Christian. Later she felt she was being "called" to be a pastor's wife. She met and married Wayne Williams, who indeed became a pastor.

Did you understand at eight years old that you would be different?

What I remember is riding home from church that day and having a fight with my sisters in the back seat of the car. I was so disappointed because I thought that I would no longer have those inclinations, to yell at my sister. I thought that would be gone!"

Many years later, T.J. has found herself a partner in ministry with her sister, Linda Gwathmey, who pioneered the San Antonio CWJC project.

We were living in Houston, where Wayne had pastored. My father became ill, and my parents were unable to manage by themselves. I was coming most weekends to San Antonio to help Linda take care of them. At the same time, our church was studying *Experiencing God,* and we came to the week when it asks something like, 'What outrageous thing do you think God may be asking you to do?' I wrote, 'Move to San Antonio,' but I didn't tell Wayne.

"A few weeks later, Wayne lost his job. We decided that if we were going to make changes, we should consider all the options. Both of us found jobs in San Antonio before we even moved there!"

T.J. worked as an office manager, volunteering more and more at the CWJC

"For we are God's workmanship, created in Christ Jesus to do good works, which God prepared in advance for us to do" (Eph. 2:10).

God is already paving the way for you to do His work! Sometimes we can only see that in hindsight. Can you look back and point to a time like that?

"Each one should use whatever gift he has received to serve others, faithfully administering God's grace in its various forms" (1 Peter 4:10).

What skills and gifts has God given you? Make a list of some ways you could be used to "administer God's grace."

center with her sister, until she really felt that she was being called to work there full time—but with no pay.

Wayne's response was, 'If I was being called somewhere, we would go; we shouldn't consider this any differently.'

"I had business skills that Linda needed—computer skills to produce newsletters, to handle correspondence and finances. Linda is the program coordinator. Women come Monday through Friday from 9:00 to 2:30 for training in reading/writing, computer, office equipment and protocol, preparation for interview, and competency exams. Volunteer Christian women mentors provide encouragement, transportation, prayer support, advice.

"CWJC of San Antonio was one of five pilot programs—the only one to add the classes to the mix. We felt that these women needed training before they were equipped for any opportunities we might find for them. The state of Texas has a law limiting the amount of time a person may draw welfare assistance. And the government is realizing that it can't do it all."

What makes the program different from a government agency?

That we care so much. You can't pay people to care. These women are overwhelmed with the love they feel.

They know that everything—every table, every chair, every piece of paper—was given by people who care, and yet have never even met them. I get a chance every day to tell them how much I care about them, to express God's love. If I worked in some government agency, I might feel stifled. Also, you can't program or legislate the power of the Holy Spirit!

"Every day we start off with a Scripture, usually a Psalm. So many of them are about the poor and oppressed and the power of God; these women can really relate to that side of God.

"I relate to God's unconditional love, but it's also my biggest struggle."

But we like to think God will call us do something we're good at.

Maybe He puts us there so that we know that it's not *us* doing it, it's God. To be Christlike is to empty yourself and let Him come in—to give Him every part of you and let Him put Himself in your place.

"This work has taken me to shelters and places I've never been before, couldn't even imagine. It makes you appreciate what you have. Every time I get into my car, I'm thankful that I have one. I used to resent doing laundry; now, I realize what a luxury it is to have a washer and dryer in my own home, to do laundry whenever it's convenient. And I don't deserve these things any more than they do; in fact,

"Such confidence as this is ours through Christ before God. Not that we are competent in ourselves to claim anything for ourselves, but our competence comes from God" (2 Cor. 4:7).

What are your weaknesses? How could God accomplish His work through your weaknesses?

some of them deserve them more than me."

Do you feel overwhelmed?

Absolutely! Today, one of our students is having back surgery—a woman who lives in a shelter—and when she is released, she'll go to the shelter to recover. I just want to take her home with me! You want to fix it for them; you have to remember that you can't fix it. Only God can."

Jesus did not spend His time in high-powered meetings, or setting up organizations. He did not build a building or amass a fortune. His days were filled with people—children, women, businessmen, tax collectors, prostitutes, cripples, the rich and powerful, the poor and destitute. They interrupted His meals, pulled at His robe, climbed on His lap, got in His face. He put up with it because they were the reason He came. And if He became impatient with His disciples or angry with the Pharisees, it was because they missed that point.

"Open your eyes," Jesus told His distracted disciples, "and look at the fields" (John 4:35). Down the road, through the fields, came the Samaritan woman, returning to the well, and following behind her were the white-haired heads of the village men who had come to see this Messiah. "They are white for harvest" (John 4:35 NAS).

There is one lens through which we must view everyone we encounter: that is Jesus Christ. If they are believers, Christ lives in them. If they are nonbelievers, Christ died for them. No one is without worth. It is entirely possible to be church-man-like and not love people—the Pharisees proved this! But it is impossible to be Christlike without it leading you to love the people for whom He came. "Whoever does not love does not know God," wrote John, "because God is love. ...We love because he first loved us" (1 John 4:8;19, emphasis mine).

The Bible tells us that Jesus could see into the heart of man (John 2:25). He knew the past, present, and future of everyone who came to Him to be healed or fed or restored. He knew this man would go home and beat his wife; He knew that woman would cheat her neighbor. He knew that many in that crowd would be with the mob and cry, "Crucify Him!" To Him, the masses of people looked like dumb, dirty, smelly sheep. But He healed them anyway. Why?

Because He loved them. It was His nature.

[1]Carter, Rosalynn, *First Lady From Plains* (Boston: Houghton Mifflin Company, 1984), 10. Used by permission of The University of Arkansas Press. All rights reserved.
[2]*Ibid.*, 15.
[3]Carter, Rosalynn and Susan K. Golant, *Helping Yourself Help Others* (New York: Times Books, 1994), 122–124. Used by permission of Random House, Inc. All rights reserved.
[4]Carter, Jimmy and Rosalynn Carter, *Everything to Gain: Making the Most of the Rest of Your Life* (New York: Random House, 1987), 191. Used by permission of The University of Arkansas Press. All rights reserved.
[5]*Ibid.*, 96–97.
[6]*Ibid.*, 23.

_____

_____

_____

_____

_____

_____

_____

_____

_____

_____

_____

_____

_____

_____

_____

_____

_____

_____

_____

_____

_____

_____

_____

_____

_____

_____

_____

_____

_____

5

Grace

Offering the Love of God

For all have sinned and fall short of the
glory of God. But God demonstrates his
own love for us in this: While we were
still sinners, Christ died for us
(Rom. 3:23; 5:8).

When I was in the sixth grade, something happened to me that has stuck
with me all my life.

My parents moved to a new town,
leaving behind the neighborhood and
school that had been my world since
first grade. I became the "new girl." And
I met Ginger and Shelley. They lived
behind me, just across the backyard
fence; they were the "popular girls" and,
oh, how I wanted them to like me.

Just across the street from our school
was a corner drugstore, the old-fash-
ioned kind with a soda fountain. Every
day after school, we would stop there
on our way home to buy a Cherry cola
(for a quarter!); and every day, Ginger
and Shelley would take me over in the
aisle beside the cotton balls to let me
know what nerdy thing I had done that
day which could make me unworthy of
hanging out with them. To this day, if

anyone says, "Could I speak with you a minute?" I get a little nauseous and feel like I'm back in the cotton ball aisle again.

There are grown-up Gingers and Shelleys. They are in the PTA and the office, the sorority and the neighborhood coffee shop. I once served on a church committee with them; it was an emotionally debilitating experience. I came home from each meeting a wreck, fast losing any shred of self-confidence. My good friend Cindy, who's met a few Gingers and Shelleys herself, stopped by one afternoon during that time with a little gift: a bag of those round cotton pads you use to take off make-up. Tied to the package was a note that said, "No more cotton balls."

Ah, grace. Simple, but amazing.

Susan Wommack

It was nearly 9:30 on a Thursday night when Susan and I settled down together in our jammies with our coffee cups, kids tucked in bed, dishes done, floors swept. We talked by phone like two teenagers for over an hour.

I will never forget the moment I met Susan Wommack. Susan is married to Chris Wommack, a long-time friend who had invited my husband, Dennis, and me to join them at a conference for Ministers of Music and their wives. We walked into the room the first night, somewhat nervous, knowing few people there except Chris. I had never met

Susan until then. I will always be grateful for and admiring of her God-given ability to make you feel like an old friend. Although we see each other only once or twice a year, it is always as if we had been together just yesterday.

Susan and Chris met and married after they were well into their careers. Chris graduated from Baylor University and was in full-time music ministry. Susan was an attorney, a graduate of the University of Texas. Susan once told me that she had been the only Christian in a secular environment for so long that it was a major adjustment when Chris joined the staff of a church. "I had to get used to Christians," she joked.

Susan, didn't you grow up in the church?

I'd grown up going to Sunday school, being there all the time, and I'd always heard how God loved me. I knew He loved me, knew He had a plan for me, knew I was precious to Him, but never had been faced with a decision to accept Him. It was as if I were already accepted; that's how it was presented to me.

"When I was a freshman in high school, I went to a youth revival held in the gym at our school. I cannot tell you what was said; it was a very simple message. But it was the first time in my life that I heard about hell. It wasn't scary to me; it put the big picture

"Love your neighbor as yourself" (Matt. 22:39).

How well do you love yourself? Do you give yourself grace? Do you know you are valued? You cannot offer anything from God to someone else that you cannot first accept for yourself.

together for me. When I heard there is a hell, and we need to make a decision, it was a lightning bolt; it was like, okay, that makes such sense to me that there's two hands to Him. There's the God of love and righteousness, but there's the God of wrath and judgment. And I thought this was a decision I had to make. I didn't cry, it wasn't emotional, it was just the most logical thing I'd heard in ages. So, the good part of all that—growing up with "God is love"—is that I have a wonderful self-identity with who I am in Christ as far as being loved and accepted and precious in His sight. That was the first foundation I had. And then came the conviction of sin. I see that as a benefit."

When I asked Susan's husband, Chris, to tell me what is Christlike in Susan, he said, "She can talk to anyone at all and make them feel valued. She talks at their level, she really focuses on them; people remember their conversations with Susan and walk away feeling special." He's so right; I have been the grateful recipient of that focus. It's as natural as breathing to Susan; I suspect she doesn't even see it as a virtue.

I wonder if that ability comes from the security of feeling your own acceptance—of feeling that you are loved, therefore you have confidence to go out and offer that to other people.

Oh, definitely. I saw that modeled very much. My dad never felt that he was more special than anybody else. He knew everyone from the bank president to the janitor and talked to them equally. He knew everything about them, he would ask about their kids; he would remember them and always stop and shake hands. So I grew up with that."

My sister-in-law grew up with a father who measured everything by performance and gave no affection or recognition unless you excelled. And she still struggles with that. The hardest thing for her in coming to God was, 'I have to get it all right before He'll love me.' That was when I realized what a foundation I'd been given in being taught from the cradle roll, 'The sky is blue; Jesus loves you.' I grew up with the knowledge that I'm pleasurable to Him; and that does make a difference in how you feel about yourself. You can go out and make other people feel as though they're acceptable, they're interesting and fascinating, because you feel that you are.

There's a book I read to my children called *Little Bear Finds A Friend*. He does not want to go to school, he's holding onto his mom's apron; and she gets down with him and says, 'Little Bear, in order to have a friend, you must be a friend.' A lot of people want a friend without making any effort. It's

"If anyone has material possessions and sees his brother in need but has no pity on him, how can the love of God be in him? Dear children, let us not love with words or tongue but with actions and in truth" (1 John 3:17–18).

What specific actions have you taken to help someone in need in your community?

hard to have a friendship without both people feeling they're important, and both people feeling special. Because of my background, being made to feel I'm important and special—feeling confident—I realize that means many times I have to go out of my way because some people can't do it. I don't understand that, because it's not my personality, but I know it exists. And the minute you speak to them and are nice to them and initiate, it's amazing the change you can see."

But you know, some people do that, Susan, and they pounce. They "pounce you" when they initiate a relationship—sort of in your face. You really have an ability not to do that; and that's an indication of your attitude that everybody has worth and can be respected. For your father to talk to janitors, he had to think they were worthy of respect. That might be one of the hardest things for Christians, especially with non-Christians: to respect their personhood. I think what non-Christians are afraid of is that Jesus will take away their personhood because they have not encountered Jesus, they've encountered a lot of well-meaning Christians who've wanted immediately to use the four spiritual laws on them. You have to earn the right to be heard; you have to know their background, something about them, not just pounce on them, lay your formula on them, and expect them to make a decision.

They have to know you're coming to them from love. They have to know, "You're sharing this with me because you care about me." I think that makes the biggest difference.

A lot of it's just the everyday natural sharing what the Lord's doing in your life. It's amazing what happens when you pray, "Lord, lead me to these conversations." You look up, and you're 15 minutes into conversation! You can't believe you're there! That just blows me away. I think, 'Wow, this is the most natural thing.' I didn't have to force it, and my heart didn't have to race. (Sometimes it does!) But because they're getting to know your heart, it just happens."

You're not just a little nervous about them getting to know you well enough to see "warts and all"?

F or me, being a Christian before the neighbors doesn't mean that we're a family without problems, it's that we're a family that does have the same problems, the same struggles, and we're going to share them with you. Hopefully, you'll see that we handle them differently. No one wants to be around June Cleaver or Donna Reed. I don't! They don't want to see someone whose life is perfect, because most of us don't live a perfect life. Hopefully they see that you're seeking the Lord for wisdom, that you're trusting Him, that you're not

"Always be prepared to give an answer to everyone who asks you to give a reason for the hope you have" (1 Peter 3:15).

Can you explain why Christ makes a difference in your life? Can you do it with words that anyone could understand?

"Do not forget to entertain strangers, for by so doing some people have entertained angels without knowing it" (Heb. 13:2).

Who could be in your backyard? A future President of the United States? The next Billy Graham? Someone who will be a teacher of the next generation?

worried, that faith overcomes the worry aspect, that you take it to the Lord.

"That's what I hope the neighbors see: that life is not different at our house as far as what happens day to day. Our focus is different and we handle things differently. And I hope when they come into our home they feel that—that you're perfectly loved and accepted. There are certain things that aren't going to happen, but you're loved and accepted here."

How are you getting that message to your kids, then?

When I was growing up, our home was not the hang-out house at all. *We* want to be the hang-out house. (Chris swears I run a day care!) I want these kids over here; I want to get to know them. Our kids do go to other people's houses, but many of the neighborhood kids are over here a lot. Most of the moms on the street work, so the kids are in day care all day. So I want a lot of them over here, because I want to know what's going on. I want to know what's being said. But I also want to offer them a place where they know they can come. My best friend's house was the hang-out house. Her parents were the ones that we went to.

I am the hang-out house, and there is, I discovered, a price tag that comes with it. I have to put up with children who don't behave the way mine behave. I have to be gracious about messes. I have to accept that my house isn't going to be neat, clean, and orderly, but everybody's going to feel comfortable that they can put their feet up. Inside I'm always battling with, 'My furniture isn't as nice as everybody else's,' but if it were nicer, I wouldn't let kids sit on it!

Especially if you get kids who have been unattended, they don't have manners, they don't know how to behave in a family. At first it was a little bit of a stretch for me to love some of those kids (or even to be nice to them!)

And sometimes you say to yourself, "Why am I training this child for someone else? That's their parents' job."

Because God put you there, my friend.

That's exactly right. Those kids are so drawn to consistency and a sense of order—and I'm not talking about order as in neatness, but as in rules and boundaries. They pick up on it, so that when they're out in the back yard and scream, 'Shut up, you stupid!' they turn to you and say, 'I'm sorry!' It's a place of love, but a place of conviction. There's a real balance there."

My friend Karen Dean says that what people want out of the church is what they got out of the show Cheers: *they want a place where "everybody knows your name"—where you walk in, and everybody says, "Norm!" Where, even if you're as nerdy as Cliff Claven the*

"Let your gentleness be evident to all. The Lord is near. Do not be anxious about anything" (Phil 4:5–6).

Is your relaxed (non–anxious) life the evidence that God is with you?

mailman, you've got a place to sit. Our challenge is to be "a non-anxious presence"—someone who is not shocked when they take off their shoes or tell us their secrets. We all need a place where we don't have to perform.

You know what amazes me? We constantly have moms and their kids over. The mother and I will have a soft drink together and let the kids play. It's a child-proof home; I'm not too worried about what they're going to do. But how many women are scared to do that with someone! They're scared their house isn't orderly enough. 'Oh, I can't have you over, my house is a wreck.' I'm thinking, 'Okay, have you not looked around?' But you see, that is the most natural thing in the world to me."

Well, it's natural to you because you've given yourself grace—because you've said, "That's not what I'm going to judge myself by." But to someone who says "Everything has to look perfect for me to be acceptable," that's very hard, because they have set this unrealistic standard. At your house, they can feel comfortable because you've said, "Hey, I've got dirt. You've got dirt. Big deal."

Exactly. My friends tease me about the state of my house, and I say, 'Where do ya'll hang out? Where do you stop by? My house. So get off my case.'"

❧

What gives you the confidence to be yourself? What's the source of your self-esteem and security? Psychologists say that a crucial factor in a healthy sense of self-worth is the knowledge that you are loved by someone. The apostle Paul, writing to the believers in Rome, wanted to make sure they knew the unconditional, unchangeable love of God. "For I am convinced," he wrote, "that neither death nor life, neither angels nor demons, neither the present nor the future, nor any powers, neither height nor depth, nor anything else in all creation, will be able to separate us from the love of God that is in Christ Jesus our Lord" (Rom. 8:38).

Alice Conner

"Blessed assurance! Jesus is mine!" wrote hymnist Fanny Crosby. "This is my story; this is my song."[1] You can always tell a person who knows the truth of those words when she sings them. Alice Conner is one of those people.

Alice is what some would call bright. She wears bright, stylish clothing and has a smile that could stop traffic. Her confidence and exuberance are contagious. As a senior director for Mary Kay Cosmetics, she inspires the same confidence and self-esteem in the women who work for her. When we met in her bright red kitchen one morning, I discovered the depth of assurance that inspires her joyous confidence.

"I know whom
I have believed,
and am con-
vinced that he
is able to guard
what I have
entrusted to
him for that
day" (2 Tim.
1:12).

*Alice, when did your assurance in
Christ begin?*

When I was nine years old, we
were in a revival, and I remember
this overwhelming feeling that 'I am sinner and I can't get to God on my own.
The only way is to understand that
Christ died for my sins, and because of
that I don't have to be separated from
God.' It was just overwhelming. At nine
years old, it was this heavy burden on
my heart. I mean, at that age, what sins
had I committed?"

*You could understand in some way as
a child that you needed help.*

Yes. I didn't understand it all then.
But I know that I was really saved
when I was nine. I think that is a
tremendous assurance, and it really
affects the way you live your life. I
don't know if that assurance came into
me then or over time. But what a
tremendous undergirding that was!"

*You just put into words something I've
never heard so concretely: the tremendous assurance to know that you're
guaranteed a life with God forever, that
you'll never lose His love. You can't
underestimate what a difference that
makes in your life. You think about it
when people die, or some horrible thing*

happens to you, but if you believe it, then it changes how you live every day; eternity starts now.

And it affects how you react to everything that happens in your life! Some people probably think I'm a Pollyanna because I have such a positive outlook on life, on the things that have happened to me—the death of a grandfather, grandmother, a close friend. Jay's mother lived with us for four years on kidney dialysis, and people said, 'Oh, what a cross to bear.' And no, it wasn't easy, but we made it through.

"We get too beaten down by life— especially women—to believe in ourselves. And that is something that I can offer to the women in my business. When they come into Mary Kay, if they will stay around me and come to the meetings, I really do believe in them, and I tell them—and that's the key. I write notes and tell them; sometimes that's the only time they hear it and they hang on it. Doesn't seem like a whole lot, yet it is."

They usually come to you at a point of need of some kind, don't they? There's a divorce, or they've lost their job, or there's a self-esteem problem.

If you meet a woman that is really sharp, and she just got a raise or promotion in her job and thinks she is the best thing since sliced bread, you are not going to recruit her into your

"I know what it is to be in need, and I know what it is to have plenty. I have learned the secret of being content in any and every situation, whether well fed or hungry, whether living in plenty or in want . . . My God will meet all your needs according to his glorious riches in Christ Jesus" (Phil. 4:12, 19).

Does your life reflect contentment regardless of circumstance?

business. She is totally satisfied. It'll be down the road when the bubble gets burst. There are lots of different needs; it's not just a money thing. It's a self-esteem thing. It can just be getting out with adults. But there needs to be a dissatisfaction of some kind in some area before they're interested."

And don't you think that's true of Christ? People are so able to meet their own needs, they're so satisfied, they don't feel a great need for God. It comes at a time when the bottom drops out for them, when they realize this is all there is, they've got everything and something is still missing. You can talk to them about it, but sometimes all you can do is live it out. You can have what you have: the joy and the resiliency in crisis, and ultimately someone will ask, "How can you handle this thing that levels me?"

Many sales units in Mary Kay have a Bible verse. Every unit has a name; most people use their last names, but I used my first name—my unit is called 'Alice's Wonderland.' So I use the symbol of the heart a lot. Our top person is the Queen of Hearts. My unit's Scripture is Psalm 37:4: 'Delight yourself in the Lord and he will give you the desires of your heart.'"

Some of our readers might think all that foo-foo stuff—giving little awards, the Queen of Hearts—is silly and trivial. It's not what's important.

It is *so* important! There is still a child in every one of us. And we all need to bring that out, we all need to laugh, to just get silly."

And I think we all need to be given gifts and affirmation. "Princess moments." When we were little girls, to get to put on the little crown and dress in front of the mirror was great. I went all the way through age-level missions organizations at church. I learned and remember all those Bible verses and missionaries—but I also remember what it was like to walk down the aisle in the white dress with the scepter and cape we received for recognition and feel the princess moment. And I think God understands that; Christ understood it. He bestowed those kind of princess moments; in fact that's exactly how He described the church—as His bride.

A friend shared with me a powerful experience she had at a Sunday school retreat where they held a wedding celebration of the bride of Christ. Each of the women was given tambourines or bells or banners to wave. My friend was dressed as the bride, veil and all. They marched through the house singing praise songs and read Scriptures from Song of Solomon. It was the first time many of them had understood how beautiful and beloved we are to Christ.

You don't get that from the world. You don't always get that from your husband or your kids. What a tremendously

"As a bridegroom rejoices over his bride, so will your God rejoice over you" (Isa. 62:5).

empowering thing to make people feel loved, cherished, special!

A nd they are special, they just don't realize it. But if somebody will tell them...

A few years ago, as I was browsing through a bookstore (my favorite pastime), I happened on a book by one of my favorite authors, Sue Bender. The words of its opening pages took my breath away:

"For as long as I can remember I have been listening to a harsh, critical voice inside me, but I've lived with it so long that I never really noticed the influence it was having on my life. I only listened, I believed what this harsh judge was saying.

"The voice passes judgement on everything I do.

"'You're not measuring up!' the judge shouts.

"I'm never sure what I am supposed to measure up to, only that I never will.

Nothing I do will ever be enough.

"'Don't complain,' the judge adds, you have it easy.'"[2]

I bought the book. I have heard that voice.

Luci Freed

The voice of the critic is not the voice of God. That is a message Luci Freed has been trying to get across to women for years—maybe because it's a message she's been trying to get across to herself.

My earliest childhood memory is playing outside, drawing hopscotch on the sidewalk. I loved the sun, feeling the warmth of it and knowing that I was loved by God. Now that was not something that was said in my family. We went to church, a very legalistic church. But somewhere in there I really fell in love with God and stayed that way.

"I wanted to go to a Christian college so I could learn about God. So I went to a college where the only people who seemed to know God carried big black Bibles and never smiled. They never seemed to be happy and didn't dress in any way cool. They looked miserable. And the rest of the people at this Christian school were pretty well partying. I didn't get it. But I knew I didn't want to look like the people with those big black Bibles.

"So about a year into this Christian school, I decided I was going to hang out with what you would call *pagans.* I can remember that we would get out of chapel and go immediately to a restaurant and drink beer. By the time I got out of there, I didn't want anything to do with God. I remember the day and time that I said to God 'Look, I have been good, and it hasn't done any good at all. I give up. I've been good, and I'm

"Blessed are those who hunger and thirst for right-eousness, for they will be filled" (Matt. 5:6).

going to be bad now.' And so I was—as bad as you can be.

"I lived in a hippie community—because they loved each other. It was like the family that I didn't feel I had; it wasn't condemning. Yes, they were smoking pot sometimes, but for a while it was the safest support system. You didn't have to be anything, you just had to be yourself. And I think that's some-thing that the church is missing. But eventually, things got bad for me, and I began to be afraid of the drugs I'd been taking. I finally moved out of there, but I just got so weak. And I thought, *I've got to have more of God.*

"Some friends of mine had been pray-ing for me. I remember calling them and saying, 'I don't even know how to pray'—and we're talking about a girl who had been raised in church. They were the first to say, 'Just talk to Him like a friend.' I'd never heard this before. So I went to their house, and I said, 'I need this God thing you've got.'

"I would spend hours reading the Word like I'd never read it—I'm not sure I ever really had read it. I would go home at lunch and read my Bible, I was so hungry for God."

Is that when you realized that to have Christ in your heart would mean your life would be different?

It meant a desire to *want* to live differ-ently. It became. 'I want to live for Him.' Actually it became 'I want to

know Him'; I didn't even think about
actions. Unfortunately, I was now going
to another legalistic church who had
lists of rules, too. And I kept those
rules, wanting to do anything to please
God, because I felt like I had made
such a mess of my life. And finally I fig-
ured out that I'd better get on with
knowing Him."

Luci Freed is the director of the Crisis
Pregnancy Support Center in Nashville,
Tennessee, which provides pre- and post-
abortion counseling, pregnancy tests,
and crisis pregnancy intervention. She is
a crusader, not just in the arena of abor-
tion; Luci's crusade is that women real-
ize how much they are loved and valued
by God.

When I worked here as a volunteer, I
was impressed with your whole approach
to abortion: that it's not that these girls
come in here needing to be talked out of
doing a bad thing, but they come in here
needing acceptance and love. They need
to know God, and then they will make
better choices; it will change the way
they make choices.

The Lord allowed me to have that
'looking for love' feeling, and I
looked in the wrong places. And that's
what's happening with the women we
counsel. Only God, the Father God, can
fill up that hole. No man can fill up a

"Everyone who drinks this water will be thirsty again, but who-ever drinks the water I give him will never thirst. Indeed, the water I give him will become in him like a spring of water welling up to eternal life" (John 4:13–14).

Where do you turn to fill your need for love? To the mall? To the refrigerator? To the gym? To the office? Do you recognize this need in others in your life?

woman's needs, and I've come to clearly see that every woman who walks in here—every woman who walks around churches, every woman at the Wildhorse Saloon—is looking for love. You might go to church every Sunday, but not know God's love and be so lonely, so empty, so needy of relation-ship and acceptance that you give into stuff that you never thought you would—until it becomes totally accept-able."

That's why we overeat, or overextend ourselves to the point of exhaustion. Out where I live, in the suburbs, there are a whole lot of women addicted to their schedule because the busier I am, the more valuable I am; I must be a good person.

In November I'm going again to Ukraine where women have had six to eight abortions because the govern-ment made them. They were forced by communists. But now that they're not forced, they don't have any money. A diaper costs a dollar, so to go over there and tell them to carry their baby to term is a whole new ball game than over here. They come saying, 'Where will I get food?' or 'My husband will leave me if I have any more children.' So they've carried their babies to term and put them in an orphanage, and now the orphanages are full. What I've been doing is post-abortion work: doing a week of healing, and training other women to continue that work.

"It's the same stuff. It doesn't matter if you go to the country club or the night club. I learned what the real ache is."

"Unconditional love! Just to accept that it's true for me. Continually I just come back and learn more and more about how much He loves me."

I think that was a key quality in Christ's life: that He knew He was loved. He knew that was the truth because He'd heard His Father say it. And He said that we, too, can know the truth. And He said, "The truth will set you free" (John 8:32). It sets you free from a lot of stuff.

Yes, including shame. One of the things in my life right now is I'm realizing there was a lot of shame put on me that I didn't know about. I knew something was wrong; I knew I didn't like me, and I thought I was a mistake, which is what shame says. Jesus has worked on it for years in me; I think I've known it and have been walking in some of it. But I've reached a new level where I believe it is sin to let shame control your life instead of God's truth about you.

"I have this memory of my mother standing over me going, 'You're bad, You're bad.' That's how I see myself, and so that's how I treat others at times. I don't just do it to me; I expect others to live up to my unrealistic, totally perfectionist expectations."

"This then is how we know that we belong to the truth, and how we set our hearts at rest in his presence whenever our hearts condemn us. For God is greater than our hearts, and he knows everything. Dear friends, if our hearts do not condemn us, we have confidence before God . . . " (1 John 3:19–21).

Shame keeps a lot of people from coming to God. Does your life demonstrate that you are free from that burden? Or are you weighed down by the same guilt as the rest of the world?

"being confi-
dent of this,
that he who
began a good
work in you
will carry it on
to completion
until the day of
Christ Jesus"
(Phil. 1:6).

What does God
want to accom-
plish in you?
Can you see
how He is
accomplishing
it?

*So, of course, God put you in a job
where you must continually offer unconditional love.*

Well, for me, it's not hard accepting clients. I guess I see myself. I have some trouble accepting men, especially men who abuse women. But it's the people who are closest to me that I have trouble unconditionally loving. I don't expect clients to be perfect; I expect my staff to be perfect. And I think they've suffered from that. But I think I also haven't gotten on my face and prayed, 'Give me Your uncondi-tional love for them.' Not until the last six months; before that, I spent all my time being critical—not just of them, but of me, too.

"One of the things I found out when I opened this center was that I didn't like women—adult women. Of course, that was because I didn't like myself, and I didn't understand that all women's prob-lems are about not knowing that they are loved by God. So I was pretty mad about that, too. And the first year we opened, we didn't see any teenagers—we saw women!

"A pastor friend of mine told me that God has a list of things He wants to accomplish in me. And so He puts me in situations where He can accomplish those things. I had a list of things I knew God wanted to accomplish in me, and one of those things was to make me a lady—an adult woman. And He has done every one of them. Compared to where I was, it's unbelievable. So now we're working on another list.

"I look back and see that God knew exactly what He was doing. I don't know anywhere else He could have accomplished this much in me."

Julie Wilson

Early on an October Sunday morning, Julie Wilson was sleeping alone in her apartment near the campus of Florida State University when she was awakened by a noise outside her front window. She looked out, but saw nothing and went back to bed. A few minutes later a man entered her room. Julie lay very still as she listened to him search the contents of her room, praying he would only steal something and leave. But he didn't. He raped her.

It was a moment that could have destroyed her life. Had it happened only six weeks earlier, it might have.

Julie, have you always had a strength in Christ that could withstand any tragedy? When did you become a Christian?

I grew up in a Christian home and went to church whenever the doors were open. I lived the basic Christian life where you just get into a routine. I remember my youth choir, the mission trips, and how much that meant to me. But you can just get into a rut of 'doing church,' and I got there eventually."

*At what point did you move from
"doing church" to a relationship? I also
confused "doing church" with what it
meant to let Christ live in me and take
over my life. Even though I wasn't a bad
person, I still lived by my own agenda; I
did not let Christ have my everyday life.*

That's what happened to me. I went
off to college and...it was funny; I
would talk about God, I was real open
about being a Christian, yet I wasn't living that at all.

"About two years later, I went to a
friend's wedding, and I know it was
then that the Holy Spirit got hold of me.
We were sitting around this table at a
country club, with five or six people I
had grown up with, who had been in
my youth group at church. All of a sud-
den, the Holy Spirit came over me, and
I longed for that relationship again, for
that experience. I told my friend Paul, 'I
think I want to go back to church.' He
said, 'Great, I'll pick you up in the
morning.'

"First Baptist Church Tallahassee was
having a big back-to-school service on
campus. I started getting involved there,
and about three weeks later they had a
big celebration. I had to work the first
night, so I came in late and sat in the
back row by myself. The group New-
song was singing a song that talked
about living on the fence. That just hit
me like a ton of bricks. That's when it
became a relationship for me.

"I went forward that night and made

that known—that I was rededicating my
life—and never looked back. From
there, I yearned to know and to learn
and study; and the Lord brought new
great friends into my life. It was easy for
me to turn away from the old stuff; I
gave all that up and really started seeking God and His wisdom. And it was
October 18 of that same year (only six
weeks later) that I was attacked.

"When I look back on it, there were
days when I was angry at God, when I
didn't sleep all night—when I look
back, I think, 'If I had been living like I
was before, I would most likely never
have gone home that night; I wouldn't
have been there for that person to break
in and hurt me.' But I also know that if
I wasn't living for God, if I wasn't seeking God by then, I would never have
made it through this. Because He was
the only thing that could get me
through. I was so committed to learning
and doing that daily quiet time with
God that I had the strength to survive."

*Did you ask, "If you love me, how
could you let this happen, God"?*

Believe it or not, I never did. Here's
one thing I don't remember, but my
mother said that the first thing I did
when I got up after my attacker left was
that I grabbed my Bible and held it to
my chest. And I said that day, 'God's
got a plan. God will not forsake me, He
will use this for good.' That's how
strong my relationship had become.

"And we know
that in all
things God
works for the
good of those
who love him,
who have been
called accord-
ing to his pur-
pose "(Rom.
8:28).

When has God
worked in a
difficult situa-
tion to bring
about his pur-
pose in your
life?

"Consider it pure joy, my brothers, when-ever you face trials of many kinds, because you know that the testing of your faith devel-ops persever-ance. Perseverance must finish its work so that you may be mature and complete, not lacking any-thing" (James 1:2–4).

Believers and non–believers have trials. The difference is in how we react to them. When you face a hardship, do you rejoice because it is a chance to grow and learn?

Thank God I was at that point in my relationship with Him that I could say that! So I never questioned, 'Why me?' I wondered how that guy picked me; but I never questioned why God allowed it to happen. I didn't feel like it was pun-ishment for all the bad things I'd been doing. I knew that God would use it, and He has—not even, I think, fully to the extent that He can or will someday. God's given me a gift—and it is a gift, I feel."

A gift? Who would ever imagine that such an awful thing could be called a gift? But then I remember the story of Joseph, sold into slavery, unjustly impris-oned, in the end forgiving the brothers who had betrayed him: "You intended to harm me, but God intended it for good to accomplish what is now being done, the saving of many lives" (Gen. 50:20). I know what God says in Isaiah is true: "As the heavens are higher than the earth, so are my ways higher than your ways and my thoughts than your thoughts" (Isa. 55:9).

My sister Leigh Ann called and asked me to consider coming to Nashville. Leigh Ann and her husband, Lanny, were getting a new house that was very conducive to having someone live with them, which is what they had offered. I thought that was great for my sister to offer, but outstanding for Lanny; that's a lot to ask of a brother-in-law. I came to live with them, and it couldn't have been easy for them.

"I was also struggling with the break-up of the guy I was dating at the time of the attack. He had moved to Atlanta, and I went to see him. I was really low and very needy. He basically looked at me and said, 'I don't love you; I never loved you, just leave me alone!' It's an embarrassing story, to have to say that you ever acted so desperate! But I did, I was so desperate. I had asked too much from my boyfriend as a result of the attack, and that's why I had lost him. So I got angry at God about that.

"But the next morning I went to First Baptist Church in Atlanta and Andy Stanley preached a sermon about trusting God at all times. He said, 'So many times we say, "Okay God, I know you're God, but you obviously don't know me, because if you knew me, you would know that this is the guy for me." And God is saying, "No, it's because I love you and because I know you that I'm saying give it to me; and if you'll give it to me, I'll give you the real thing."'

"My tears dried up that day. Growing up in church we hear 'trust God', but it was the way he said it—as if God had told Andy he had to preach that sermon that morning because Julie was going to be there. And it was a process. I had to give it to Him. I had a lot of healing to do.

"When I first went to Nashville, Leigh Ann introduced me to a woman she knew who had been attacked about 20 years ago; this woman was a Christian and had offered to help if there was anything she could do. She took me out to lunch, and I was able to get a Christian woman's perspective on the healing process. She said to me that day, 'I look back, and I wouldn't change a thing,' and I said, 'I can't imagine that day ever coming, but I hope it will.' Of course, it didn't even take me twenty years. In fact, it was when I met my husband that I realized I wouldn't change a thing, or I wouldn't have him. I think back and know that if I had not been attacked, I might never have left Tallahassee, gone to Nashville, or met Tad. So God even used that for His purpose."

Today, Julie and Tad Wilson live in Columbia, South Carolina, where Tad is Minister of Youth at First Baptist Church. They have a new baby boy, their first child, Taylor.

I credit it all to the strength of my relationship with God that I didn't go through so much hate and anger. In fact, I used to get mad when people would tell me, 'Oh, just wait. You're going to crash one day and hit rock bottom.' And I would think, 'You don't understand the strength I have behind me, not my strength; it's God's strength.' I didn't like being told that God wasn't strong enough to get me through it. I didn't have to hit rock bottom, and I didn't have to hate or be angry all the time; I didn't have to let it ruin my life.

We tap so little of the power available to us—any of the resources available to us in Christ. If you were coping with this under your own strength, Julie, of course you would crash eventually. I have a friend who was healed of cancer, and people keep waiting for it to come back. She says, "Why can't you just accept that I was healed, that God can do that?"

"You have heard that it was said, 'Love your neighbor and hate your enemy.' But I tell you: Love your enemies and pray for those who persecute you" (Matt. 5:43–48).

I know! He's done more miraculous things! You know? I remember I worked in the attorney general's office when I was in college. They had Victim's Rights weeks, and one day they were showing videos of rape victims talking about their attacks. I don't know why I wanted to go, but I did. On the video, one woman had cut all her hair off because the man had pulled her down the stairs by her hair. All the women were angry and devastated, their lives were over, and they were miserable. I went back up to my office crying, and I called Leigh Ann and said. 'I don't want to be like that ten years from now.' She said, 'You don't have to be. You have something those women don't have; you have God.'"

Do you ever pray for your attacker?

When I was still living in Tallahassee, I was driving down the road and the realization came to me—it was so awesome!—that I wanted this person who attacked me to know God and to have Christ in his life. I mean, none of us would doom anybody to hell on purpose! And it hit me that if he became a Christian, he would go to heaven. And although I might say, 'I think I know that guy,' we would walk down the streets of gold together and not have hatred for one another. That's the power of God and His love and forgiveness. And my forgiveness—to say, 'Yes, sin is sin, and some of it scars us more than others. And this guy certainly put a kink in my life, but we can walk down the streets of gold together and not remember what happened.' That was a very awesome thing to me, because it just showed God's love."

Is that the most significant quality of Christ to you? His love?

Yes, maybe because I just had a son—that He died for me. If I had been the only person on earth, He still would've died on the cross. To think that God gave up His son for us, that's real to me, when I look at my son. Jesus knew all along that He would have to die for our sins, and He didn't want to do it, but He did. I just think how much Jesus loves me, no matter what I do—that He'll always forgive me, and it's forgotten. It's just so simple! I feel like I sound trite, but…"

It is simple. I never realized how that foundation of truth—the unconditional love of God—was a foundation upon which to build a life. It changes your perspective on everything that happens. Sure, at some time we all doubt it and wonder if He really loves us no matter what. But even when you strayed away from it, Julie, it was planted in your heart.

Yes. And the Holy Spirit truly did a work in my life to bring me back. Having had a son, it becomes very real; I wouldn't sacrifice my son for anybody. Knowing that God did that for me is incredible."

It is incredible, literally: hard to believe, impossible to prove. Except that when you look at someone like Julie, you are looking at living proof of God's grace and forgiveness. And if we can believe He can love us like that, mustn't we also believe that He loves the ones who hurt us? Do we dare believe that He could even love them through us? That is the incredible truth. Until you know that truth and it becomes a part of you, you will never be free.

As Julie put it, "It's not like I introduce myself with, 'Hi, I'm Julie. I'm a rape victim.'" It happened to her, but it doesn't define her. What could have been a life scarred forever by evil instead bears the unmistakable imprint of the hand of Christ. It is the hand with a nail scar. It is the mark of grace.

"Very rarely will anyone die for a righteous man, though for a good man someone might possibly dare to die. But God demonstrates his own love for us in this: While we were still sinners, Christ died for us" (Rom. 5:7–8).

¹Crosby, Fanny J. "Blessed Assurance," *The Baptist Hymnal* (Nashville: Convention Press, 1991), 334.

²Bender, Sue, *Everyday Sacred* (San Francisco: HarperSanFrancisco, 1995), ix.

6

Simplicity
Living to Please God

*The one who sent me is with me...for I
always do what pleases him* (John 8:29).

I grew up in Texas, where football is
big. My friend played football. He says
that one of the best things about the
game was the roar of the crowd and the
sound of the announcer echoing in the
stadium, "Number 36 goes in for the
play!" He says it was many years later
before he realized that he still went
through life listening for the roar of the
crowd and the commentary of the
announcer.

Whose voice are you listening for?
Who does the commentary in the background of your daily life—your mother
or father, your spouse, your teacher,
your boss, your friends? Who is your
audience? We all play to someone.
Whom do you live to please? "And a
voice from heaven said, 'This is my Son,
whom I love; with him I am well
pleased'" (Matt. 3:17).

Jesus listened for one voice: His
Father's. Many other voices called to
Him, each with its own agenda. The
crowds wanted Him to perform miracles. The disciples wanted Him to inau-

gurate an earthly kingdom. His family wanted Him to come home. Jesus was constantly listening for what His Father wanted. Jesus ate, drank, and slept for His Father's purpose. It was as natural to Him as breathing. It was the reason for every decision He made, every response to everyone He encountered, every movement, thought, and action. Pleasing God was not something Jesus did in addition to His everyday life; it *was* His everyday life. It explains why He acted and why He at times did not. It explains His timetable and His priorities. It explains His inexplicable behavior. It explains why He was different.

Claire Cloninger

My friend Claire Cloninger has long been on the fast-track of the Christian music industry. She is the award-winning lyricist of songs that include Wayne Watson's "Friend of A Wounded Heart," Sandi Patty's "Friendship Company," and B.J. Thomas's "You Gave Me Love When Nobody Gave Me A Prayer." Her lyrics appear in hymnals. Claire is the creator and lyricist of numerous musicals for church choirs, a gifted speaker, and the author of several books, including *Postcards From Heaven* and *A Place Called Simplicity*. Her life seems anything but simple!

Claire, have you always loved God?

I always had a heart for God even though I didn't know Him, but my personality fought with my spirit. I had a chronically restless nature. (Is that what they call 'human' nature?) Wherever I was, I felt there must be 'a better party down the street.' Whomever I was with, I was sure there was someone more interesting I could be spending my time with.

"But it wasn't until I was grown with children of my own that I heard the rumor that Jesus Christ was interested in having a one-on-one relationship with me! A group of Christians from Houston came over to our small, rather stuffy, traditional church in Louisiana to do a series of teachings and Bible studies. They were the most amazing people I had ever come in close contact with. In our church we referred to the Savior as 'Christ our Lord.' They knew Him by His first name! They called Him 'Jesus,' and they were madly in love with Him. I'll admit I thought they were a little weird and fanatical, but I also secretly thought they were wonderful. Their joy was very real and very compelling. I found I wanted what they had. So one night when they led a prayer to invite Christ into our hearts, I made that spiritual transaction and knew that I had stepped over from death to life.

"But very little changed in me. If anything, I got worse instead of better. I don't think I ever really knew what a temptation was until I was a believer.

"Since, then you have been raised with Christ, set your hearts on things above…not on earthly things" (Col. 3:1–2).

What do you long for and think about?

(Satan doesn't have to tempt you if you're already his.) I began to read the writings of the women's movement. I became very self-absorbed, looking high and low for that job, hobby, avocation, relationship which would bring the fulfillment to my life that I thought I deserved."

How many "if onlys" have I entertained? If only I had that job, or that house, or that dress, or that opportunity.

Contentment is a significant difference in a believer's life; not too many of us have it. We live in an insatiable culture. What the world does not need are "Christians" who exhibit the same hunger for power, possessions, success, and pleasure; it needs people who have found the source of contentment, acceptance, and security it so desperately seeks—and who live differently because of it.

The struggle between being like Christ or like the culture is a daily battle. It is very subtle because we are surrounded by the culture on all sides, and we are not surrounded by very many Christians who are sold out to God."

Yes; when my sister-in-law, Kim, was struggling with the decision to follow Christ, she said to me one day, "Here's what I don't get: the people at church don't seem to be much different than the people anywhere else." (A sad indictment.)

"Well, Kim," I said brilliantly, "you can't look at the church to know what God is like!"

As soon as the words were out of my mouth, I realized how absurd they sounded! Kim was giving me that "Okay...and your point would be?" expression.

"Then where do I look?" she asked.

"You look to Jesus." That's what I told her. Second Peter 1:3 tells us that in Christ we have everything we need for life and godliness.

One night I got my Bible down, and in a desperate game of "Scripture roulette" I flipped through the Bible and found Psalm 37:4: 'Delight yourself in the Lord and He will give you the desires of your heart.' I realized I didn't even have a vague notion of what my heart desired. But that was when the Lord assured me that He knew my desires. He knew because He had made my heart and programmed those desires within me. He actually knew what would fill my emptiness and still my restlessness. And it was Him.

"That night I did more than profess my belief in Jesus. I put Him in control. And that has made all the difference. My life has not been easy. It has been far from perfect. But the major change for me is that the restlessness is gone. I am no longer looking for "a better party." If

"The fear of the Lord leads to life: then one rests content" (Prov. 19:23).

you know Jesus, you are at the party. He is real life. As Peter put it in John 6:68, 'Lord, to whom shall we go? You have the words of eternal life.'

"What I really desperately needed at that initial point of my journey was someone to disciple me. I was an infant requiring guidance."

I don't think we realize how much we need a spiritual mentor, someone who has been down the road before us. Especially when we aim to please God, we need somebody to point out to us, gently or not-so-gently, "Hey, you're way off-track."

In the theater, there is a term called "giving someone the hook." It means that if someone is on-stage flubbing his or her scene or going on too long, someone offstage takes a big hook and jerks that person off the stage! Well, I believe that God gave me the hook right after I surrendered my life to Him. I was into so many things right about then—volunteer work of all kinds, amateur theater.

"God gave me a special friend named Virginia to disciple me. Virginia convinced me that I had signed up for an "all or nothing" kind of life when I gave Jesus the reins. She felt that God needed time with me to get my heart in tune with His, and that would require my getting out of everything for a while. Virginia advised me to fulfill every obligation I was under first, to honor every commitment. Then I was to withdraw quietly.

That sounds like a dream—to actually say no to obligations. (My friends have threatened to make me wear a "Just Say No" button!) How did you ever do it?

Believe it or not, it was not difficult to do. I felt my need of God so keenly that it felt easy and right to get out of all those other things. So I finished everything and got out, and for two years I didn't do anything much but take care of my family and study the Bible with two other women. It was during that time that God began to give me songs—songs that would later lead me into the fulfilling career that my heart had longed for!"

I've noticed that pattern in almost everyone God used in the Bible—Moses, David, John the Baptist, Mary, Paul ...even Jesus. They all spent time out of the center of activity, preparing for the moment He called them into action. He knew the exact moment when they would be ready.

That's what He's working on in me. He is teaching me to be content on the sidelines instead of in the spotlight. He is teaching me to go with His agenda, not to push ahead with mine. It goes against the grain, but it is healing.

"My mother laughed when I wrote my book, *A Place Called Simplicity.*

"But seek first his kingdom and his righteousness, and all these things will be given to you as well" (Matt. 6:33).

Does this verse mean put Jesus at the top of your "to–do" list? No, it means to put Him at the center of your life, and let everything else revolve around Him. How would that change your present lifestyle?

"'How can you call your life simple?' she asked. 'You are on a plane twice a month, flying off to some speaking engagement or other.'

"She is right. My life is not totally tidy or wrinkle free. One mistake many of us make is to view simplicity as 'learning to do things more efficiently in order to be able to do more things.' This is not simplicity. It is exactly the opposite."

*It is doing **less** that matters **more**. Simplicity is shaking off a culture that says, "You have to" and replying, "No, I don't."*

Trisa Usrey

Trisa and Kyle Usrey live in China, where they teach English, law, and business.

I could not speak with Trisa openly about her work while she was in China. We chatted by email several times in a crude kind of code. When she and Kyle returned to the US for a few weeks, we spoke by phone, and I finally got to hear how her love for Christ led her to say "no" to her own culture and "yes" to a culture half-way around the world.

Trisa, how did you and Kyle end up in China?

Kyle was working for a huge law firm out of Chicago with an office in Denver. He was making 'six digits,' as they say, and I was court-reporting for a federal judge; we were very comfortable, needless to say. But you know there's always that little degree of dissatisfaction; you're just not quite where you want to be. After a year and a half at the firm, Kyle realized the price to be paid for that income was your sanity, your health—anything that they wished to exact of you. And so he said no. He just told them, 'My family (which was just me) and my energies are going to be eroded in the way that you are using me.' They were very unhappy, but he went to work for McGraw Hill, the publishing company.

"In the winter of 1993, Kyle became very ill with something that to this day is undiagnosed. We just don't know what it is. He was unable to dress himself, barely able to speak and sometimes unable to walk. He was so sad. But he slowly, slowly recovered. It took a long time, a total of probably a year. In the midst of that, he was so distraught, and he asked, 'What does God want of me?' I said, 'Well, you need to ask Him.' He did, and the result was that Kyle decided to contact an agency that finds organizations that are looking for believing Christians to serve in a particular area of expertise or education or experience. You purchase 'possibilities' from them for something like $25. For three months, we were deluged with literature. We were awash in wonderful opportunities! And somewhere in about

"Choose for yourselves this day whom you will serve, whether the gods your forefathers served beyond the River, or the gods of the Amorites, in whose land you are living. But as for me and my household, we will serve the Lord" (Josh. 24:15).

Have you made a conscious choice between the "gods" of the land in which you're living and the Lord?

the middle of those three months, I
remember Kyle calling to me from the
bedroom in back, 'Hey, honey, here's
one! They want to send us to China to
teach!' and I said, 'Well, you know
where you can file that one, big guy.
I'm not going to China.'

"I should've learned not to say that by
my age.

"He didn't throw the file away, of
course, but filed it with lots of other
promising things that had potential; but
as Kyle continued to become more and
more well, he sort of forgot that he'd
told God he'd explore what God
wanted for him.

"A year later, in January 1994,
McGraw Hill sent Kyle to a business
meeting in Washington, DC. He was in a
hotel on Capitol Hill; he was coming
down from his room on something like
the 35th floor. On the elevator were two
gentlemen. Kyle glanced over and read
their name tags—and they were from
the agency that sent us the overseas job
profiles! (Kyle had followed up on that
first piece of literature and said, 'Send
me what you have.' So they were aware
of us, but we didn't know how aware
until this elevator incident.)

"He said, 'I know your organization,'
and they said, 'How do you happen to
know?'

"He said, 'Well, I wrote away for
some literature.'

"The two men said, 'What is your
name?' He said 'My name is Kyle Usrey,'
and they said, 'Kyle! We have been

praying for you.' They said, 'We're having one of our Canadian-American fundraisers, a big annual meeting in the hotel. Why don't you join us and get some more information?' So he went with them to their meeting room, and they handed him lots of information.

"Kyle said, 'You know, what you're doing is so great; but I'm trained in the law. I have a degree in law and business, and I'm confident that's what God wants me to use in however God wants me to use it.' And they said, 'Kyle, this year, for the first year in our agency's fourteen years in China, one of the universities has asked us for a lawyer.'

"Well, poor Kyle, he was so scared, he ran up to his room, slammed the door, braced a chair against it, and hid!"

You can't hide from God that easily!

Really! After the business trip, he came home and told me about it. I thought, 'Oh, man, I've got to sit up and take note; this sounds serious.'

"So, we began to pray about it. The agency did a follow-up phone call to ask, 'What are you thinking? What's God saying to you?' We said, 'Well, nothing clear and nothing definitive yet.'

"They called in October of that same year and said, 'We are going to have a meeting of alumnae from your area, Colorado Springs, and we want you to come.' We said, 'Sure,' and put it on our calendar. It was our usual psychotic day, where we raced to work, raced home,

slammed down our dinner, raced to
meetings at consecutive hours: one at
6:00, one at 7:00, and one at 8:00.
Theirs happened to be the 8:00 meeting,
so of course we were running late!

"We were so late and so lost that we
called them from a gas station and said,
'We can't find your meeting place, and
we know you've already started without
us, so we'll just catch you next time
you're in town.' One of the men in the
elevator, said, 'Kyle, we will wait as
long as it takes for you to get here.'
Kyle came back to the car, and he said,
'I guess they're going to sit there all
night if we don't go talk to them.' So we
tried again, and this time we found the
townhouse.

"There were about ten people there
who had been in China and returned,
most of them several times. They went
around the room sharing briefly what it
had meant to them and how their lives
would never, ever be the same. Then
we watched their most recent film—
about a 15-minute film. It showed on-
site work in the classroom and around
several communities in China, interviews
with teachers, and interviews with Chinese students. And the film was the cat-
alyst. The Holy Spirit spoke clearly and
loudly to both of us. Kyle was already
feeling convicted, of course, after that
elevator experience! I was much less so,
but certainly available to God's instruc-
tion. So when the lights went up after
the film in this home, all these ten people were passing their tissues around

because they were so homesick for China—but no one noticed that we, too, were weeping.

"We left without making a commitment, but I would say within hours that night—we talked long into the night—we felt this was what God wanted for us. So, then came the matter of divesting ourselves of everything—of things to which we had emotional ties and physical ties.

"We'd wanted to go that way anyway. We attend what I would describe as an upper middle socio-economic-group church, and we were getting more and more dissatisfied with our own complacency—how easy it was to just go along and not do anything for God. So we began to sell things and give things away. We gave notice at our jobs. We each quit our jobs three months before we were to leave for China, closed our bank accounts, sold all the various equipment that we used in our employment, stored what we wanted to keep in the homes of friends, and got ready to go."

That is really literally what Jesus said: "Sell everything and come after Me" (Matt. 19:21).

He said to take just a cloak, and we took a little more than that, but there was not a more liberating feeling in the whole world than to have made that decision. There was no pain and no fear—the pain of leaving our friends,

"No one can serve two masters. You cannot serve both God and Money" (Matt. 6:19–24).

How available are you to serve God? Are you already a slave to money and possessions?

but no pain of divesting ourselves of a culture we had allowed ourselves to be sucked way into. We knew this was what would gladden the heart of God, and we didn't want to stand before God with only what we had to show up to that moment."

I heard a young couple speak recently who were preparing to leave for North Africa as missionaries. They said, "Pray that we will be able to live at the level of our new culture. We want to be one of them, but we know we are so adjusted to American culture that it will be a shock. Pray that we will not be discontent."

I'm quite sure that somewhere in the back of our American minds, it nags at us Christians that this is not the way the church is supposed to operate. When I read the passages in Acts about the early church, I think, "That's not what we're doing."

Interestingly, we just finished studying Acts with our new believing students in China. (We've had 16 students receive Christ.) Kyle and I would be almost shaken when the Bible study would end, because we realized how far we had digressed from that model and how ashamed we were. On the other hand, we just rejoiced with our new little sisters and brothers in our university, because it's going to be a lot easier for them! They're undeveloped! And they're so communal-thinking anyway, that we think this is going to be much more

akin to the life that they already know—
the communal way of life—the way of
life that is described in Acts, of caring
for one another and dividing things
equally. They almost do that now; their
motivation is different. They do it for
survival, and they do it because they
have no choice; it is a behavior that is
dictated to them. But now, they have
Christ as a motivation and live with all
the joy that He can give you when you
obey Him! We're just really excited to
see what happens with them in their
own little community."

*We live, in America, under the mis-
guided impression that our country is
still a primarily Christian nation. It isn't;
and it's becoming, it seems, increasingly
harder to remain Christlike in the American culture than in some other cultures
around the world.*

I'm convinced you're right. A little
hunger would go a long way to getting us back to depending on God!"

*So you've come back to the US for a
few weeks. Is it a culture shock, even
only having been in China for only eight
months?*

Yeah, it's kind of overwhelming. I
didn't think it would be quite so
much so after just eight months. We
were in Boulder, Colorado, and we saw
they have a nice lovely mall. And I
thought, 'I don't know where the

"Don't let the world around you squeeze you into its own mold" (Rom. 12:2 Phillips).

How are you being shaped into the pattern of the world? Pray to grow more and more in the image of Christ.

darkness is greater—in China or in the Boulder mall!' But, oh, the food and the money that's being outlaid hither and yon. Even after a couple of days, I said, "'Kyle, we've got to leave. I can't believe it; I'm already getting a yen to buy totally useless things. How absurd!' So I haven't been cured completely, I'm embarrassed to say.

"To tell you the truth, Karla, I have a real fear about returning here permanently. What am I going to do, pretend like my year and a half, or two years, or three years in China never happened? Am I just going to step right back into American culture and pick up where I left off, accumulating things and doing very little good in the eternal sense?"

Do you really feel you can do very little good if you come back? Are we all going to have to do what you and Kyle did in order to please God?

No, I don't believe that, not for one minute! So, I guess my unhappiness is just with me. I fear myself!

"Those are things I'm still struggling with. But the thing that I keep firm in my mind is that I have been called; my call was crystal clear, and I hearken back to it when things are bad and when things are good. That keeps me focused and on the path, and I'm grateful, so grateful that God could get me to the point where He could reveal His plan for my life. If there is ever any one area in which I want to reach my highest potential, it is in telling the good news."

Hebrews 11 contains a list of names often called "The Hall of Faith." Like a hall of fame tour, the writer walks us past heroes of our faith: Abel, Enoch, Noah, Abraham, Sarah, Jacob, Moses, Rahab, Gideon, David. These were all commended for their faith, says our tour guide, for "without faith, it is impossible to please God" (Heb. 11:6). Without faith, we cannot cut loose the strings of our culture, as Trisa Usrey did. We cannot step forward into the unknown.

"Let us throw off everything that hinders and the sin that so easily entangles us," urges the writer of Hebrews, "and let us run" (Heb. 12:1). You cannot run and drag along the baggage of your past. You cannot run encumbered by the weight of your own dreams and plans. You cannot run and stay comfortably where you are. You cannot even run in your own strength; you must fix your eyes on Jesus, "the author and perfecter of our faith" (Heb. 12:2).

Marijean Green

Marijean Green is a strikingly beautiful woman, with dark hair and huge dark eyes. She is the same tiny size she was the day I met her, more than 15 years ago. She is the wife of the highly-respected and successful Christian music artist Steve Green. Having traveled literally around the world with Steve's ministry, Marijean now remains at home with their two teenagers: daughter Summer and son Josiah. Her life appears about as picture-perfect as anyone could ask; but on the afternoon we sat in the corner of her living room, Marijean was quick to dispel that image.

Marijean, when did you start struggling with perfection?

I was raised in a Christian home. I can't remember a time when I didn't know who Jesus Christ was. I grew up in the church and had Christian parents. I always tried to be perfect and to please everyone. But at age nine, I realized I couldn't be perfect. I heard verses like "All have sinned and come short of the glory of God" (Rom. 3:23), and I realized that I was a sinner, and I couldn't fix it. I realized how much He loved me for the very first time. He wasn't waiting for me to be perfect; He just wanted me to be His."

That's interesting coming from you, because the public who knows you and Steve through his ministry must think you pretty close to perfect. You mean, you aren't?

Because much of our life is public, there are a lot of people who know very little about us. They only see the magazine covers and read brief articles about our lives. They know us from a distance. But we do have close friends who have walked with us for many years and who know us intimately. That's really the place of greatest comfort and safety: to be in a relationship with those who are committed to helping us grow up in Christ.

"As far as being the perfect family—there is no such thing. All of us are broken people in need of a Savior. The only hope we have is to receive all that Christ has given us and ask Him to mold us into all that He wants us to be."

You said that you grew up trying to please everyone; I did, too. How did you come to understand what pleasing God meant in everyday life?

Although I've known the Lord for a long time, I still struggled with a performance mentality. If I did well, God would be pleased. If I messed up, He would be disappointed with me. So much of our life is based on performing. Early on, we're praised for good behavior and scolded for doing wrong. We get As for superior school work and rewarded for our achievements. By the time I got to college, I had excelled in most areas. I was president of the choir, a leader in National Honor Society, voted "best all-around girl" in my high school. I was an "A" student. I had performed well and been rewarded. Everyone liked me; I thought God must

"For you know that it was not with perishable things such as silver or gold that you were redeemed from the empty way of life...but with the precious blood of Christ" (1 Peter 1:17–19).

"Be wise in the way you act toward out-siders; make the most of every opportu-nity" (Col. 4:5).

Think of three opportunities you have in the course of your daily routine to witness by the way you act towards some-one who is not a believer.

certainly be happy with me, too.

"Before long, I was involved in beauty pageants and ended up in the Miss Florida pageant. All my supporters knew I would be one of the finalists, or maybe even the winner. When I didn't make the top ten, I was crushed. I had failed and disappointed all those from my hometown who had invested so much in me. Knowing that was almost more than I could bear.

"A few years later, I developed an eat-ing disorder. I was more concerned about looking good and being accepted than being spiritually and emotionally whole. Bit by bit, my perfect record was crumbling; my performance was failing. All this was God's kindness, letting me come to the end of myself to see the sinfulness of my heart.

"That's why the gospel is such good news! I am fully accepted in Christ. Someone once said, "Cheer up. You are worse than you think. And cheer up. You are more loved than you dare imagine." Christ was perfect *for* me. He *is* my righteousness."

The first time I met you and Steve we were in Alexandria, Indiana, at a recording session. That was when Steve's career was really taking off and he had major opportunities. He was also at that horrible age of early twenties, when you think you're God's gift to the world! But later, I saw you two begin to reject that ambitious way of life that many artists— even Christian artists—follow.

It was a conscious choice to reject that way of life, but in response to God's working. Steve was literally rescued. He had been resisting God and drifting farther and farther away from Him. Even though Steve was raised in a godly home on the mission field, he had returned to the US with a rebellious heart. It wasn't until five years into our marriage that God got hold of Steve and powerfully changed him! As a result, we set about to order our lives by God's Word. Not only our marriage and family, but our calling in music as well. Steve was very concerned about building a strong foundation. He didn't want a career that was man-made by marketing and promotion; he wanted to be sure God was in it. Some people thought we were crazy because we had asked his booking agent not to make "cold calls" (asking churches if they would let him come to sing.) We wanted to go only by invitation, where there was an open door and open hearts. Then, we chose to travel as a family, home-schooling our children and living out of suitcases for ten years, to keep our family close.

So, it was a choice of where to put your confidence, not just a choice of lifestyle.

I was thinking this morning of that verse 1 John 2:15-17: "Don't love the world or anything in the world. If anyone loves the world, the love of the

"Do not be
overrighteous,
neither be over-
wise. Do not be
overwicked and
do not be a
fool. It is good
to grasp the
one and not let
go of the other"
(Eccl. 7:16–18).

Father is not in him. For everything in
the world—the cravings of sinful man,
the lust of the eyes and the boast of
what he has and does—is not from the
Father, but from the world." And I
thought, "What does that mean, to love
the world?" It's the spirit of the world, is
what he's talking about."

*Wanting to fit in? Wanting the same
things?*

Right. And so I've had to ask, 'How
does that relate to me, as a wife, a
mom?' Am I going to run after material
things, just like the world would do, or
am I going to be more concerned with
eternal things? Am I going to be more
concerned about how I'm fulfilled, or
am I going to put myself into my children, in training them, and give myself
away? Just that whole thing of spending
my time on temporal things versus eternal things. To love the world would be
'think temporal.'"

*But you do look like you have it all
together, Marijean. I mean, I see you at
the grocery store with your kids when
you're not "on," when you're not "Marijean Green, public person." I know it's
not just an image.*

*Big tears well up in Marijean's dark
eyes. She lowers her head for a minute.
There is silence. When she finally speaks,
it's in a whisper.*

Well...anything good in me—anything—is because God has worked that in me. God has so worked in my life over these years. My very life is dependent on Him, I can't do anything without Him. And because He loves me, He keeps me there. I can't be a good Mom, I can't be a good wife, I can't be a good friend unless I am empowered to do so."

She points to an arm chair in her den.

That blue chair over there is my spot; that's where I have my time alone with Him. The Lord shows me my own heart, my need for Him, and then I ask God for direction for the day: 'I don't even know how to spend this day if You don't show me. I'm going to spend it on worthless things; I'll go to the temporary every time unless You steer my heart in the right direction.' I keep a pad and pencil nearby, and He begins to show me things that are important.

As I read His Word, I think of practical ways to apply what He's showing me: a letter to write or sometimes just things that need to be done, people I need to pray for."

I think people assume God only wants to talk about religious things, that He's not interested in their to-do list, when He is very interested in it. That's probably why it keeps coming to mind when they sit down to pray.

I think so! As children of God, our whole life is sacred; every part of our day is lived in the light of His presence. So even the ordinary things have divine meaning.

"Really when it comes down to it, our lives are not our own. I mean, who do I belong to? If I think that I'm just here for me, that's a dead-end road. It brings nothing but selfishness and death, eventually. I know that in myself. The only joy I ever get is giving my life away, serving others. So I must have the attitude in the morning, "I do not belong to myself; everything I have belongs to You. You are sovereign; orchestrate my day the way You want it." If I don't do that, I'm not ready—I'm not ready for the opportunities He does bring. I mean, God has just shown me, He's going to give me plenty of opportunities.

"And I was thinking this, too: that when I come to the Word, I come to more than a page; I come to a person. Do I come with the attitude that 'Whatever You show me today, I am going to obey?'"

Doesn't that wreak havoc with the plans you've made for the day?

Yeah! A lot of times my plans get changed. And I have found that if I just give it up—give up what I want to do—that the Lord gives me joy in doing His plan. It's when I fight against it that I get frustrated. That's God's grace to let me know that my plan is not going to be fulfilling; His plan is always going to be more fulfilling. It happens all the time! Because you always have "interruptions," but you look at them and ask, 'Is this phone call an interruption?' Or do I say, 'This is an opportunity?'"

Doesn't it bother you when you go to bed and things didn't get done?

It used to, really. Now I'm trying to have the attitude of relinquishing my right to myself and surrendering. It's just a dependence on the Lord. And there's rest in that.

There's never a time when you can say, "I'm off" spiritually. But there is a time, well all the time, when you should sit back and say, "it's not up to me; it's up to Him."

Yes. My existence is to glorify Him, just to glorify Him in whatever that is."

"I have brought you glory on earth by completing the work you gave me to do" (John 17:4). Those are the words of Jesus as He spoke to His Father in the Garden

"Give me understanding, and I will keep your law and obey it with all my heart" (Psalm 119:34).

James 1:5–8 tells us to ask for wisdom, but not with a doubting heart. If God gives you the wisdom you ask for, are you prepared to obey it?

of Gethsemane. Actually, the work had not yet been completed; the cross and the resurrection were yet to come. But in His heart, it had already been completed. Christ had settled the question of Who He lived to please. He was already listening for the voice of His Father saying, "Well done."

7

Submission

Obeying the Will of God

*For I have come down from heaven not
to do my will but to do the will of him
who sent me* (John 6:38).

I know you've already decided you
don't like this chapter. I used the "s"
word, the one many women shudder to
hear: *submission.*

I was in a women's Bible study once
where the verse "Wives, submit yourselves to your husbands" (Eph. 5:22)
actually provoked anger. Otherwise-
normal women, my friends, got red in
the face and trembled. As my mother-in-
law says, "They got huffy." Just the
mention of submission is like a finger-
nail scraping across a blackboard. It
goes against our grain. We've been well-
indoctrinated by our culture that submission is an admission of inferiority or
weakness. I am Woman; hear me roar.

Before you say, "Amen" and skip on
to the next chapter, let me remind you
of two things: First, Paul also had a
command to husbands: "Husbands, love
your wives just as Christ loved the
church and gave himself up for her"
(Eph. 5:25). Submitting to be loved like
that doesn't seem so bad!

And second, shuddering at submission

is the mindset of our culture. And we are not citizens of this culture.

"Your attitude should be the same as that of Christ Jesus: Who, being in very nature God, did not consider equality with God something to be grasped, but made himself nothing, taking the very nature of a servant, being made in human likeness. And being found in appearance as a man, he humbled himself and became obedient to death— even death on a cross!" (Phil. 2:5–8).

Ouch!

Don't skip this chapter. If you do, you will miss learning about the very heart of Christ and what He expects of us.

"For I have come down from heaven not to do my will but to do the will of him who sent me," Jesus said (John 6:38). We spend a lot of time in the church wondering about God's will. "What is God's will? How can I find God's will?" If you're uncertain of God's will, you have to look no further than John 6:40 (emphasis mine): "For my Father's will is *that everyone who looks to the Son and believes in him shall have eternal life.*"

If this is big news to you, don't worry; you're not alone. Contrary to what many Christians believe (and teach), God's primary agenda is not that we be happy or prosperous or fulfilled or successful. God does have an agenda: that everyone on earth may see Jesus, believe in Him, and have eternal life. When you and I became Christians, *we offered our lives up for that purpose.* Were you aware of that when you accepted Christ? I wasn't. I thought I now had God's help to accomplish my agenda. It has come as somewhat of a shock to me to discover over the years that I'm not in charge.

"There is a God," one of my favorite T-shirts reads, "and you're not Him."

Dellanna O'Brien

I first came to know of Dellanna O'Brien when I was a little girl. At that time, she was a missionary in Indonesia, and I prayed for her regularly. Today, Dellanna O'Brien is Executive Director/Treasurer of Woman's Missionary Union®, Auxiliary to Southern Baptist Convention. In her position, Dellanna is responsible for leading approximately 1.1 million women, girls, and preschoolers in missions education, mission support, mission action, and personal witnessing. The path of her life has taken some surprising twists and turns since the first time she submitted it to God for His purpose.

You learned about Christ at home, right?

I was one of the fortunate ones born into a Christian home, and as a result made my profession of faith in Jesus at the age of seven, a very early age. When I was a teenager, I had a significant spiritual experience. Looking back on it, I believe it was the time when I

"If you love me, you will obey what I command" (John 14:15).

Did you understand this when you became a Christian?

recognized that my commitment at age seven was even more important than I had thought it was. I realized that following Jesus was more that just saying I loved Him—it meant a commitment of life and to obedience that only a more mature person could recognize."

"Why do you call me, 'Lord, Lord,' and do not do what I say?" Jesus asked His disciples (Luke 6:46). Perhaps John was remembering these words when he wrote, "We know that we have come to know him if we obey his commands. The man who says, 'I know him,' but does not do what he commands is a liar, and the truth is not in him. But if anyone obeys his word, God's love is truly made complete in him. This is how we know we are in him: Whoever claims to live in him must walk as Jesus did" (1 John 2:3–6).

It's true that most of us who become Christians at an early age don't understand the full impact of our decision. We understand that God loves us and we love Him; that's the basis for the relationship, but it's just the beginning.

Can you remember when you first realized the decision to commit your whole life to Christ would make your life different?

I didn't interpret that decision as being a call to any kind of special service.

But, I think I did realize that it meant something more; it meant that God would use me in the future if I were available.

"When I was in high school most of my friends were Christian, many of them Baptist, and so while my choices were in keeping with a Christian's life, it didn't necessarily call for a real choice. But in college, people with whom I related were from a larger focus, and I realized that to be a Christian meant doing some things—not just not doing some things. I found Christians who were far more mature than I, who had set their sights on being available for what I later knew was a missions lifestyle. They opened my mind and heart to the significant things that a Christian could do in following the Lord that would make a difference in His kingdom."

What's been your biggest struggle with submission?

That has to be patience to allow Jesus to work in my life and in a situation in His timing. As a result I always want to do something, and it is hard to be willing to wait for His leadership and timing."

That's the tough issue for me, too—timing. Most often, obedience is not so much a question of what to do, but when to do it. One of my favorite songs by Randy Thomas says that we must wait

"But I trust in you, O Lord; I say, 'You are my God.' My times are in your hands..." (Psalm 31:14–15).

What are you waiting on God's timing for? Are you taking matters into your own hands?

"Shall what is formed say to him who formed it, 'Why did you make me like this?' Does not the potter have the right to make out of the same lump of clay some pottery for noble purposes and some for common use?" (Rom. 9:20–21).

Are you willing to let God shape you into whatever He needs to use?

on the Lord to find out what He wants for us. His timing is what is important. If we wait on Him, He'll tell us what to do, what to say, and where to go.[1]

What impresses me about your life, Dellanna, is your willingness—both yours and your husband Bill's—to make some pretty major adjustments, sometimes in response to God's call for Bill and sometimes in response to God's call for you. That must be a real juggling act. And it must require relinquishing any agenda of your own.

When Bill and I were married and he felt a call to the ministry, it required that I be willing to follow. Each time Bill was called to a new place, we made that decision jointly. As a result, even though the move hinged upon a call to Bill, God always provided ministry for me. I never once felt that I was being deprived in acting on Bill's call.

"Although I grew up in a very active Christian home, somehow I never felt called to the missions field. It was when Bill and I were at Wilshire Baptist Church in Dallas, and Bill was in the seminary, that God placed us in the presence of foreign missionaries. For the first time, we began to sense God's call. Not only did they give their testimonies that made us pause and consider that we might serve as missionaries, but He revealed where He wanted us to go as a result.

"When we were considering mission

service, however, the Southern Baptist
Foreign Mission Board (now called the
International Mission Board) required
that both husband and wife respond to
a personal call to missions. For the first
time, I dealt with being sure that God
was calling me as an individual into His
service. After being on the field for a
while, I realized how important that
was. The difficulties we faced were
accepted because we both felt that God
wanted us to be there as a team. And I
was an integral part of the ministry."

*After eight years as Southern Baptist
missionaries to Indonesia, Bill and Dellanna returned to the United States. Bill
served as executive vice president of the
Foreign Mission Board. Dellanna
resumed work in elementary education
and administration and later became
president of International Family and
Children's Educational Services.*

When we came back to the United
States, I no longer had a Christian
ministry role as a professional and so
once again was reliant upon Bill's call.
However, when Woman's Missionary
Union (WMU) Executive Director's
search committee asked me to consider
becoming the executive director, once
again I was placed in a position of
determining God's call to me. It was
one I was unwilling to consider inde-
pendent of Bill's participation. The two

of us together struggled through the time when we were sifting out God's next step for us."

The opportunity required a move from Richmond, Virginia, to Birmingham, Alabama. It also meant that Bill's career would take an unexpected turn.

I can never adequately express my gratitude for a husband who is willing to allow God to speak to his wife, and to be a part of a decision that would place his own call in the background. Thus, we entered into a new kind of relationship together as a couple and before God. We both learned that God never really deals with just one in a husband/wife team, but with both individually and together."

Dellanna accepted the WMU position, and the O'Briens moved to Birmingham in 1989, where Bill is now director of the Global Center at Beeson Divinity School, Samford University. They have three grown children and six grandchildren.

What about your children? Were you ever afraid for them, or did you regret what your obedience also cost them?

We never hesitated about taking our children. (However, Denise, who was seven at the time, really had questions about taking her little sister, Erin, who was only two. Denise said, 'She can't tell anybody about Jesus!')

"We knew when we went to Indonesia that when the children were in high school they would have to go to Singapore and live in the missionary kids' hostel there. We thought that would be a long time in the future. When the time came to send Denise away to school, it was so difficult. She was so young, but God was good to give her everything she needed to cope in her new independence. And He even gave us peace.

"While we were in Indonesia there was an attempted communist coup. We, of course, were concerned about the children's safety. It is in these situations that you acknowledge that God loves your children even more than you can. We all learned the lessons of reliance and dependence upon Him.

"Through the years, roles have changed but call has not. Our call to be obedient and to be God's children involved in His mission continues to be the goal for us. As a result we have had an exciting, joyful, and fulfilling life of service. He wants more for us than we can possibly want for ourselves."

But what if He wants our children?

Susan Carter
Susan Carter is an editor of children's Sunday School materials at Lifeway

"The Lord will accomplish what concerns me..." (Psalm 138:8 NAS).

Do you trust that God will take care of all the details involved in what He has called you to do?

Christian Resources in Nashville, Tennessee. She and her husband, Bob, are actively involved in their local church. Bob has served as chairman of the deacons. Susan teaches Sunday school and sings in the choir. Susan, Bob, daughter Candi, and son Scott are what you would call "good Christian folks." Susan grew up in the church and was ten years old when she became a Christian. She told me about that experience.

The pastor came over and we sat on the front porch. (I can still see us on Sunday afternoon.) He wanted to be certain that I understood."

That you understood what?

That Christ was my Savior, that He died for my sins, what it meant to accept Him—that it meant having a lifestyle that was different, that I truly understood it wasn't just walking down front, shaking the pastor's hand, and being baptized. So through the years I was so confident that I had a life-changing experience, that Christ really was my Savior and that He was Lord of my life. I never, ever have doubted that experience. I was really sure of it."

Many of us think we're really sure about our salvation if Jesus has always been a part of our lives. Or because Christianity was taught to us as a child.

Or because we had a powerful, emotional experience at salvation. But there is a knowing, a surety that only comes out of obedience—when your faith is put to the test.

In 1995, Susan's son Scott committed to two years of service as a missionary journeyman to Singapore.[2]

When God interrupted your life with plans for Scott, it sort of threw you off, didn't it? But didn't you always raise Him to listen to God?

Yes! Our pastor Mike Glenn said it best in the commissioning service: 'We tell the children to go, but then when one does, we say, "Not mine!"' And he could not have expressed it better for me."

Did you ever expect it would be your child?

When Scott was involved in an active youth group, at one point he had mentioned ministry. But then he was taking economics classes in high school, and one of the field trips was to Wall Street. After that, he did a total turnabout. He was going to go into finance of some type—banking, stockbroking, or something of that nature. He never mentioned the ministry again."

"In his heart a man plans his course, but the Lord determines his steps" (Prov. 16:9).

I first met Scott Carter when we traveled with a team of missions volunteers from our church to conduct sports evangelism and backyard Bible clubs for two weeks in Dundee, Scotland. He was your typical young, ambitious, good-looking guy. He'd just bought a shiny new black Jeep Cherokee; he was on his way up in the bank. He had the world on a string.

He had decided to major in business at college. He finished in three and a half years because he wanted to be on with life. He was always very focused. So he decided that he would come back home and stay with us and save money and get a job at a bank. He had worked there for about six months when the opportunity for the Scotland missions trip came up. He had a week's vacation, and he wanted to go. I knew he was interested in the missions trip; I also knew that he loved golf, and this was a chance to see the famous St. Andrews course!

"But I saw that serious side of him in his commitment to the Lord that I had seen when he was in high school. I could see the spiritual growth. And when he came back from Scotland, he was a very different person.

"When we left on the plane to London, Scott got out his journal and started writing in it. We teased him for writing about every detail, even his plane ride. By the end of the trip, when he showed me entries in his journal, he was seriously dealing with God. You could see it happening to him. And when we were leaving, in that train station in Dundee, I saw it. He could hardly leave. God was working on him, and he was scared!

"And when he came back and suddenly he's saying he might want to be a missionary, I had questions. When you see this big of a change in just ten days, you wonder is it just emotional? Is it for real?

"At first he didn't share a lot. I think he was confused, and he wasn't sure what was going on. He said, 'Well I think maybe I'll go to seminary, and I know that I want to be a missionary.' And I played the devil's advocate, trying to get him to think it through, but probably to the extreme that it was my insecurities that I wanted to settle—especially when he decided to be a journeyman in Singapore, as far away from home as you could get! He wouldn't be coming back for two years. Part of it was the mother instinct in me, but a lot of it was just lack of faith and having my own plan for his life rather than letting God plan it out.

"One of the things that made me truly realize how serious he was happened one night when I asked, 'Well, what will you do about the Jeep?' and he said, 'I'll sell it. It's only a material thing. It doesn't matter at all.' I'm thinking, 'A month ago we couldn't wait for it to come.' That was a real big clue that he was serious.

"You believe that there is one God. Good! Even the demons believe that—and shudder. You foolish man, do you want evidence that faith without deeds is useless?" (James 2:19–20).

Is God requiring you to back up your "lip service' with faith in action?

"It was really a growth process for me, because I thought, here I'd given lip service to this faith; I had put it into practice at times, but never in a situation like this."

That's what I call "erasing the page." Most of us, in determining God's plan for our lives, make a list of our own plans, hand it to God and in effect, say, "Here it is, God. Feel free to add anything I've left off."

In truth, when we offer our lives to Christ and invite Him in, we "erase the page." We hand Him a blank page, with no agenda, and we sign our names at the bottom and say, "Here it is, Lord. Whatever You want to write on it, I've already said yes."

Scott would say, 'Don't you have enough faith?' and I wanted to say, 'I do in most things, but this is really hard.' The thing that helped more than anything else was the night that the Scotland mission team got together, and I heard Scott tell the whole thing, not just in bits and pieces. How could I not be thrilled beyond words that my son was strong enough and courageous enough to totally do an about-face and change his life? So after that I had this great peace that this was what he was supposed to do; God would take care of him."

That would be the hardest for me—to resist saying, "Okay, God...but where's he going to live, and who's going to be his friend, and what happens if he gets sick?"

Of course he was not in one of the remote areas like some, but still he was far away. Yet there was a peace about it that was really hard to explain. We had a home cell group that had been praying for Scott to have a special friend, and he had several. His first caretakers were cousins of a member of our church! From the minute he arrived, he had surrogate parents—the first Christmas, five families invited him to their houses. It was wonderful. Several of them have said, when we went over to visit, 'I can't imagine what it would be like for my child to be halfway around the world on Christmas.' So they were extremely kind, concerned, and loving.

"Scott kept saying, 'You've just got to have faith.' And it finally dawned on me that if he can have this much faith, why can't I? I'm supposed to be older and wiser."

Maybe he was at an easier place to jump off. And he probably jumped without thinking about a lot of the consequences that you were thinking about.

That I felt it necessary as a mother to think about!"

Once he got over there, he probably thought, "Okay! Who am I going to be

"Therefore I tell you, do not worry about your life, what you will eat or drink; or about your body, what you will wear...who of you by worrying can add a single hour to his life? ...Your heavenly Father knows that you need them" (Matt. 6:25–34).

friends with, and what's going to happen
to me over here?"

In fact he did on the plane. When he
had a layover in Tokyo is when it hit
him, 'Where am I going?' But he followed through."

What is it Henry Blackaby says? "Obe-
dience is costly to you and to those
around you."³ Scott's decision cost you
too.

But the rewards have been far greater
than any cost. Because the cost
would be very selfish, if I were to say it
cost me anything, because it has taken
me to a new level of my relationship
with God. So the child became the
teacher!"

Jesus Himself struggled with the cost
of obedience, in the garden of Gethse-
mane. It strikes me that His prayer in the
garden—"May Your will be done" (Matt.
26:42b)—is almost exactly the response
of his mother Mary in her own moment
of costly obedience—"May it be to me as
you have said" (Luke 1:38b). I know that
Jesus was God, and so He was more able
to obey than I am, but it didn't hurt to
have a mother that modeled that. And
I've often wondered, how long did it take
her to get to that point? My friend Eve
Sarrett says a mark of spiritual maturity
is that it takes me less time to get to that
point of surrender.

A nd it comes through not only spiritual maturity, but also seeing times He's been faithful and being able to call on those experiences and remember."

Our culture tells us that we're supposed to have a plan and be in control. One of the first questions we ask our children is, "What are you going to be?" So this mysterious way of living with Christ in us—which is "take me this way or that way"—is totally at odds. But I think that's a difference that people notice.

A t one point in Scott's senior year of high school and college, I began to worry that he was becoming too concerned about materialism, salary, and career...which is everything you're thinking about in college. And for him to totally do a reversal, God had to have done a work in him."

On June 16, 1997, his journeyman service done, Scott came home with plans to attend seminary in the fall.

Is Scott's call to ministry easier to swallow now? Are you less anxious?

I think so, because I've seen that we did have our faith tested, we trusted, God took care of Scott then, and surely

"The man without the Spirit does not accept the things that come from the Spirit of God, for they are foolishness to him..." (1 Cor. 2:14).

If you truly live by the Spirit of God and not the spirit of the age, your friends or family may not understand your decisions. Can you accept that?

He'll continue to. There are still anxious moments. But there's a much greater peace.

"I think one of the most significant qualities of Christ was His willingness to give up everything for us. And I see that's really what missionaries like Scott have to try to have, too."

And their parents.

Yes. And their parents."

Christ's obedience proved that He was the Son of God. By obeying, Jesus gave God the opportunity to prove His power, even over death. Obedience is crucial evidence of Christ in our lives. When we obey, we give God the opportunity to prove Himself to those around us.

That's great, you say. But I'm afraid God will ask me to do something I can't handle.

He sure will. He will ask you to do something only He can handle.

Sally Johnson

In December 1988, Sally Johnson became HIV-positive as a result of being raped.

I had returned home from taking my three children to school and settled in my favorite rocker for my quiet time.

Instead of using my usual devotional book, God led me straight into His Word to 2 Corinthians 1:3–11: 'Praise be to the God and Father of our Lord Jesus Christ...who comforts us in all our troubles, so that we can comfort those in any trouble with the comfort we ourselves have received from God. For just as the sufferings of Christ flow over into our lives, so also through Christ our comfort overflows...Indeed in our hearts we felt the sentence of death. But this happened that we might not rely on ourselves but on God who raises the dead. He has delivered us from such a deadly peril and he will deliver us...as you help us with your prayers.'

"I didn't know at that time why God had given me that particular passage or what He was preparing me for, but I went about my day thinking about it and trying to find specific application. Before that day was over, three men forced their way into my home and raped me. I found out later all three men had AIDS and that I was HIV-positive.

"My initial reaction to the news was, 'No! God would not do that to me.' I began to realize that God's ways are not our ways; the bigger picture He sees is what really matters.

"There are so many examples of just that very thing in the Bible. My favorite is Paul and Silas in prison in Philippi. I'm sure when they got up that morning they didn't say, 'Wow! What a great day to be beaten almost to death and thrown into the darkest dungeon. I can hardly wait!' They just went about their day willing to be used of God. God saw the bigger picture of the Philippian jailer whose heart was ready to receive the message of God's love, mercy, and grace, and God needed someone to tell him. So He had Paul and Silas put in the right place at the right time to accomplish just that. He knew they would be faithful, and they were.

"The important part of the whole thing is that God had prepared me that morning. He provided the answer to *why*: These things happen so that you might rely on God and not yourself. And He gave me direction for my life: Now you are to comfort those in any trouble with the comfort you have received from God.

"I feel that He saw a great need for someone years down the road who would be willing to reach out to those in rural east Texas who are infected with or affected by HIV/AIDS. He began preparing me for that journey. First, He had to allow me to experience it and be willing to learn of Him."

Before you start thinking Sally is a saint, she is quick to say she was very afraid of God's plan for her at the beginning.

I began to 'test the waters,' so to speak, of those around me. I talked with them about AIDS in general and realized by their response of fear and horror I could never risk telling anyone I was HIV-positive. I immediately thought about my family and what might happen to them, and the real possibility of being asked to leave my church family. I let fear take over. This decision stopped God's hand short. How could I comfort anyone with the comfort I had received from God if I never told them what had happened to me? I wonder how many more like me sit silently in our churches?

"As God so wonderfully does, He showed me 2 Timothy 1:7: 'God has not given us a spirit of fear, but of love and power and self discipline.' I knew I had a choice to make: Do I continue to act based on how I feel, or what I know God wants me to do?

"God was saying, 'Do you trust Me?' I knew I had been telling Him He could not take care of me or my family, He did not know what was best for me, and He did not have a better plan and purpose for my life. Just like when I was a little child and reached for the security of my earthly father's hand, I reached my hand to my Heavenly Father, and He held on tight as we began the journey. He told me this was His ministry, not mine, and it was His strength that would hold me up. I knew I would be dealing with people whose lifestyle I would not agree with, and He reminded me He did not call me to change anyone's behavior. He just wants

"When I am afraid, I will trust in you. In God, whose word I praise, in God I trust; I will not be afraid. What can mortal man do to me?" (Psalm 56:3–4).

Who are you afraid of?

"It is not the healthy who need a doctor, but the sick.... For I have not come to call the righteous, but sinners" (Matt. 9:12–13).

Are you trying to change someone's behavior, or are you introducing them to the One who can change their lives?

me to be faithful to plant the seed of His love and grace; He will do the rest."

How did He lead you into the work you do now?

God began to show me those in my county who were living with HIV/AIDS and the fear of what would happen if others found out. They range in age from infants to senior adults, male or female, all socioeconomic backgrounds, all cultures and races. There are homosexuals, IV drug users, prostitutes, sexually promiscuous teenagers and adults, victims of sexual abuse, those who contracted it 'through no fault of their own.' The majority are infected with the virus as a result of a choice of behavior. They chose to be involved in this risky behavior and the consequences are now a matter of life and death. So they deal with guilt, anger, frustration, fear, helplessness, hopelessness."

And rejection.

Often rejection. What is interesting to me is that AIDS is the only life-threatening illness where rejection is a major fear. (We do not refuse to help a person who has lung cancer because he chose to smoke all his life.)"

How do you help?

Ihave a food pantry at my home for those with AIDS. Some of the churches help with food, especially the much-needed personal items, paper products, and cleaning products that food stamps will not buy. I provide transportation to and from the doctor, pick up prescriptions, do hospital visits, but most of all I am a friend—one who listens, cries with them, laughs with them, takes children to the park for some normalcy in their life, provides a meal, watches a movie, goes on a picnic, reads a book, just invests time and self. I have two support groups, one for family members and friends of persons with AIDS (PWAs), and one for PWAs themselves.

"This is a ministry of 'loving them' into a relationship with Jesus Christ. Some PWAs have experienced their greatest rejection from organized religion. They do not have a clue what a relationship with God through Jesus Christ is all about, because no one has ever lived it out in front of them. They see religion as only rules and regulations, not the love, mercy, and grace of God. Just as Jesus demonstrated by His life how much He loved us, we must do the same if we claim to be Christlike."

Sally, what do you mean by the term "Christlike"?

Ihear many people say 'I want to be just like Jesus' and then spend all their

"For God did not send His Son into the world to condemn the world, but to save the world through him" (John 3:17).

God's purpose should be our purpose: to save, not to condemn. What message does your life convey?

"Dear friends, do not be surprised at the painful trial you are suffering, as though something strange were happening to you. But rejoice that you may participate in the sufferings of Christ, so that you may be overjoyed when his glory is revealed" (1 Peter 4:12–13).

Are you surprised by suffering? Are you resentful, or can you rejoice that God has a chance to demonstrate His glory?

time and energy trying to copy His specific actions. What Jesus did is summed up in the one statement 'I do or say nothing except what my Father tells me to say or do' (John 8:28). If I just yield to the leadership of my Heavenly Father in everything I do as Jesus did, then I will be truly Christlike. He then will be able to do in my body some of the same things He did in His own body 2,000 years ago—touch, heal, love, forgive."

You make it sound so simple. It couldn't have been, not at first. How did you get through it?

I was angry, hurting, confused. I wondered what I had done to deserve this. Was God angry at me? Hadn't I been through enough in my life already? Being raped affects all of your being— let alone being HIV-positive.

"He has brought wonderful prayer warriors and great encouragers into my life. The warm hugs and sharing of laughter and tears are such a blessing to me. Most of all though, I am learning what a friend I have in Jesus. I am more convinced than ever of the absolute necessity for us as children of God to read the Bible daily and pray without ceasing. Reading the Bible and allowing the Holy Spirit to reveal what He has for us to learn right now prepares us for whatever God chooses for us to go through.

"God's promises are so wonderful—

especially His promises that He will
never leave us or forsake us (Heb.
13:5). But God is also teaching me His
not-so-popular promises, such as: 'In
this world you will have trouble' (John
16:33); 'Consider it pure joy whenever
you face trials' (James 1:2); 'You will
suffer as my Son suffered.'"

*I recently read in Philippians 1:29,
"For it has been granted to you on behalf
of Christ not only to believe on him, but
also to suffer for him." I have to confess
that I shrank from this truth.*

I strongly believe there are modern day
Jobs. We know that the battles are not
against flesh and blood but against spiritual forces. I believe God and Satan still
have conversations where God says,
'Have you considered my servant?'(Job
1:8). These times grow us and prove to
Satan the power of God in our lives.
God wants the world to see Him, and
for some reason He chooses us to show
them.

"I shudder when I hear someone
plead to God for Him to remove the difficult situation in their life. I have come
to learn to cooperate with it and allow
God to use it to bring glory and honor
to Him. I have seen Him do it so many
times.

"Debbie was a young woman in her
early thirties who had chosen a lifestyle
of IV drug use which led to prostitution.
She lost her husband and three children
as a result and had not had contact with

"I consider that our present sufferings are not worth comparing with the glory that will be revealed in us" (Rom. 8:18).

Which do you value more: your comfort, or God's glory?

them for twelve years. She had had AIDS for 7 years when I met her, and had become very ill. She had made a mess of her life, but in time, she saw that God could make it new. When she gave her life to the Lord, what a change—from a worm to a butterfly!

"One day I was taking her to the doctor. She was so weak I had to support her with pillows in my car. We hardly spoke a word for about half the trip. Suddenly she turned to me and said, 'Sally, I'm so thankful I have AIDS.' It took me by surprise, and I started to cry. I asked her how she could say that. She answered, 'If I didn't have AIDS, I never would have met you. And if I hadn't met you, I wouldn't know how much Jesus loves me.'

"Oh, my! The first thought I had was, 'Lord, is this my Philippian jailer? Is this the one you prepared me for all this time?' If Debbie was the only one who ever trusted Jesus as her Savior and Lord, it would be worth the trip. One of the last things she told me before she died was that she would be waiting for me by the gate. I can hardly wait!

"Oh, Karla, I could go on for pages with examples of the joy of learning of Christ and joining Him in His sufferings. It is not about being 'special' or a 'super saint,' just wanting to be all God wants us to be, and praying He is seen in us."

Sally's husband David made these comments to me:

*"Our usual first question, 'Why me?'
should in reality be, 'Why not me?'*

*"What greater honor could be
bestowed on a child of God than to know
that God, at this very moment, could be
saying to Satan, 'Have you considered
my servant, Sally?' There is absolutely
nothing in Scripture that would lead me
to believe that this scenario is not being
played out every day in the lives of thou-
sands of Christians."*

"For to me, to live is Christ and to die is gain....Yet what shall I choose? I do not know! I am torn between the two: I desire to depart and be with Christ, which is better by far, but it is more necessary for you that I remain in the body" (Phil. 1:21–24).

Life and death are so different from God's perspective. If my death will bring more glory to Him than my life here on earth, He will allow me to come home. Each night I go to bed longing to wake up at the feet of Jesus. But when I open my eyes and see I'm still here, I know God is not finished with me yet; He has given me one more day to make a difference in this world for Him.

"It can be a very exhausting and lonely ministry, and at times I have wanted to quit and find something less emotionally draining, but that is when God reminds me this is His ministry. When He called me and began prepar-ing me, He also provided me with all I will ever need to see me through. I have lost 17 of my AIDS friends in the past two years. Praise God, five have accepted Jesus as Savior and Lord, and we will spend eternity together.

"I was with one of my friends in ICU before he died. I had been reading to him from the devotional book *Streams in the Desert,* when he took my hand, looked me straight in the eyes and said, 'Sally, I don't want you to die like this.'

"As I was driving home I, too, cried to my Heavenly Father, 'I don't want to die like that!' And I remembered that His Son asked Him the very same question (Matt. 26:39). My challenge is to join Jesus in the rest of that prayer: 'Not my will but yours be done.'"

Pastor Mike Glenn taught me an important lesson from Philippians. "You have asked me how I'm doing," Paul wrote to the Philippians from his prison cell. "You've asked the wrong question. The question is: Is the gospel being advanced? If the answer to that question is yes, then I am doing fine."

¹Thomas, Randy, *We Must Wait (On The Lord),* (Maranatha! Music, © 1983).
²The Journeyman program is a two-year missionary appointment by the Southern Baptist International Mission Board.
³Blackaby, Henry and Claude King, *Experiencing God: Knowing and Doing the Will of God,* (Nashville: Sunday School Board of the Southern Baptist Convention, 1990), 136.

8

Power

Releasing the Spirit of God

*Now to him who is able to do immeasur-
ably more than all we ask or imagine,
according to his power that is at work
within us, to him be glory in the church
and in Christ Jesus throughout all genera-
tions, for ever and ever! Amen.*
(Eph. 3:20).

"All authority in heaven and on earth
has been given to me," Jesus told His
disciples (Matt. 28:18). "But you will
receive power when the Holy Spirit
comes on you" (Acts 1:8) The daily life
of the early believers as described in
Acts was filled with healing, signs, miracles, boldness, and remarkable courage
in the face of death. These were inexplicable apart from the power of God,
imparted to them when the Holy Spirit
was given at Pentecost. The early
church was not a place for wimps!

"I tell you the truth," said Jesus, "anyone who has faith in me will do what I
have been doing. He will do even
greater things than these" (John 14:12).
Does that make you nervous? You're not
alone. Like Sheriff Jimmy Brock in

David Kelley's television series, *Picket Fences*, we think there's a God, but we don't necessarily want to get in the same room with Him. Get too close, and you'll be consumed. You won't be able to control it.

I once had a Sunday School teacher explain the Holy Spirit by comparing His power to an electric current. It's there, inside the walls, all the time. When we need His power, we flip a switch, just like turning on the lights, and the power is there.

As J.B. Phillips said, "Your God is too small."[1]

People want a little bit of God— enough that we can manage, that makes us feel good about ourselves. We like to think we can tap into Him if we come to a place where we are in need. In fact, we say it: When I come to the end of my rope, I go to God. That may be true for non-believers, but once we have invited Christ into our lives, we no longer need to live like that.

Loni Pryce

I have always translated *strong* as "capable, self-sufficient, invincible." From my friend Loni Pryce, I have come to understand the definition of strong as "resilient"—able to respond to what life brings you without it doing you in.

ҿ🪶

Loni, do you think of yourself as a strong person?

I think at the core of me I am a strong person. I don't take credit for that. I don't think I have made myself a strong person; for some reason I feel that God has shown Himself to me in a special kind of way. I don't know why."

Hold it! Right now our readers are thinking, "What is that? What does that mean? I wish He would do that for me."

I'm not sure it's something I can put into words. It is the deepest inside feeling that you can imagine. There is a joy in me that I didn't put there. There is an anticipation inside me for what is to come that is strong. That's certainly not an intellectual thing; it's a gut thing."

I wonder if some people have more of a sense that this is not the world we belong to. Some people seem less at home in this world or attached to it than others. Loni has weathered a lot of crises: her brother's illness, her father's death from cancer. A little over a year ago, Loni was in a debilitating car wreck, her car rolling over, injuring her legs, back, ribs, and pelvis. Maybe that's why she's not so attached to this world.

"Sometimes you get to that place when you just hurt so bad. The worst

"Now we know that if the earthly tent we live in is destroyed, we have a building from God, an eternal house in heaven, not built by human hands...Now it is God who made us for this very purpose and has given us the Spirit as a deposit, guaranteeing what is to come" (2 Cor. 5:1–9).

Do you belong more to this world, or the next?

"In quietness
and trust is
your strength"
(Isa. 30:15).

time for me was when my dad was
dying. That was the worst that I have
ever hurt."

Worse than your own wreck?

Without question. This was just
physical suffering. When my dad
was dying I felt like I was ripped on the
inside, and the helplessness....

"I got mad at the brain tumor—the
disease that was taking away my dad.
I'm still mad four years later. I did not
get mad at God, because I trust God.
God knows what He's doing. He has all
of us who let Him, He has us in the
palm of His hand. And that doesn't
mean that we're not going to get brain
tumors, and it doesn't mean we're not
going to roll our car over. It means it
doesn't matter if those things happen,
because the bottom line of life is not
physical; it's spiritual. And God is in
charge of that—and who better? So, I'm
not saying that I go through every day
carefree, but I go through every day
knowing that the bottom-line gut-level
of life is not broken bones or brain
tumors or the fact that I can't buy a new
dress. The bottom-line gut-level reality
of my life is the spiritualness of it, and
God keeps that right here in His hands
all the time. All the time."

*Did you ever pray for your dad to be
healed?*

Yes, I did. But I also knew that did not necessarily mean taking the brain tumor away so that he could be with us. Again, God knows what's best."

My husband, Dennis, and I went to see Loni in ICU just after her wreck. We were standing outside in the hall, when a woman came off the elevator looking lost. Her name was Bonnie, and she was, as it turned out, the woman into whose yard Loni's car had flipped over and crashed. As Loni had hung upside down, her legs pinned in the wreckage, Bonnie kept talking to her while two men worked to free her. As it "just so happened," Bonnie was a believer.

Bonnie told us, "I said to her, 'Honey, do you believe in Jesus?', and Loni, hanging upside down, croaked out, 'Oh, yes, ma'am, I do!' So I shouted back, 'Well I'm going to pray for you! Call on the name of Jesus, there's power in the name of Jesus!'"

I don't know how people do it who don't know that Jesus has been through it and He's with them—because I couldn't by myself."

In Ephesians 1:18, Paul writes, "I pray that the eyes of your heart may be opened, so you can see the greatness of his power available to believers—the same power that raised Christ Jesus from

I can do everything through Him who gives me strength" (Phil. 4:13).

Do you believe God can give you His strength to get through anything? How do you know this?

*the dead!" (paraphrase mine) We utilize
about a thimbleful of the power available
to us for everyday living. I can't imagine
what we could stand or survive if we
really allowed some kind of resurrection
power loose. Most people think that kind
of power is scary!*

*But Loni's not afraid to venture into
the unknown, to go beyond her own
strength. Less than a year later, after
months of lying flat on her back and
enduring excruciating physical therapy,
Loni went to Poland as part of a volunteer missions team.*

The thing I liked about my trip to
Poland is that I could concentrate
almost exclusively on God and what He
needed for me to do. I had fewer dis-
tractions in Poland. I didn't have to go
to work, care for my house, pay the
bills, do the laundry."

*And these things you do every day.
Can't God also use you at home to do
what He needs to do?*

To an extent. I feel like I'm limiting
Him."

*And you weren't limiting Him in
Poland because you were on a missions
trip. You expected Him to work.*

And I was more available. When I say that I limit Him, I mean I limit His use of me. When I was there, I mean, I went out into this humongous public square—just walked out there, turned on the tape recorder and started singing 'You can depend on Jesus.' And I thought to myself, 'You know what? I wouldn't do this in America!'"

You just have to hear Loni sing to know what must have happened in that Polish public square. Loni used to sing in nightclubs, belting out Judy Garland and Liza Minelli tunes. When she sings "Cry Me A River," you just want to lay down and die. And when she sings about God, there is a power unleashed that is almost palpable. Offstage, she is introspective and soft-spoken. She is the living embodiment of the phrase, "Still waters run deep."

It was just so cool to be that uninhibited for a time. People gathered around and clapped along. That was quite something. Some people will, I guess, do that sort of thing. I'm not one of those people.

"It's scary for me—to show what I know. Because for one thing it scares other people, makes them uncomfortable. And there is a segment of the world that seeks out soft people and preys on them. I mean, look what they

"I came to you in weakness and fear, and with much trembling. My message and my preaching were not with wise and persuasive words, but with a demonstration of God's power, so that your faith might not rest on men's wisdom, but on God's power" (1 Cor. 2:1–5).

did to Jesus! And I say 'soft' in a good way, meaning 'open to love'—vulnerable. I think in this society we value hardness, and we are comfortable with people we don't think we can hurt."

We think that to be strong means, as you said, to be "hard"—unable to be hurt. But that's not it at all, is it? Strength is more about being able to bear hurt.

A nd that comes from knowing Whose hands you're in."

"I lift up my eyes to the hills," wrote the psalmist. "Where does my help come from? My help comes from the Lord, the Maker of heaven and earth" (Psalm 121:1–2). This psalm is one of the "Songs of Ascent"—hymns that were sung by the Jewish people each year to encourage themselves on the long journey to Jerusalem for Passover week. Scattered among the hills surrounding the city were many other temples erected to the gods and goddesses of their time. The words of this Psalm served to remind the worshipers Who was, and is, the one, true source of power.

Where does your help come from? One of the distinctive differences in the life of a believer is readiness to admit inability to self-help. "In fact, I will boast in my weakness," wrote Paul, "For when I am weak, then God is strong" (2 Cor. 12:10, paraphrase mine).

Pam Callaway

The day I called her, Pam Callaway was feeling like the worst mother in the world. "Why would you want me?" she wailed. "I'm a failure as a mother and a failure as a Christian!" Well, that's precisely why I would want her. It is her feelings of inadequacy that lead her to rely on God's power to accomplish things. This is a very Christlike quality.

"I tell you the truth," He explained to the Pharisees. "The Son can do nothing by himself; he can only do what he sees his Father doing, because whatever the Father does the Son also does" (John 5:19).

I read Philippians 4:13, "I can do everything," and put the period there. I forget the rest of the sentence, which is the point: "through him who gives me strength." If Jesus, who is God, attempted nothing by Himself, what should I attempt? Exactly what Jesus did: nothing.

Pam Callaway began to sense Jesus working in her life when she was a child.

I was six years old when I first went to my parents and said, 'I want to accept Christ as my Savior.' And they said, 'You're very young. You need to think about this. We're not sure that you understand what you're doing.' By the time I was eight, I had convinced them that I really knew what I was doing, accepted Christ as my Savior and was baptized. But I fell into a pattern that a lot of people do when they get to college: I began to slide. I went to a Baptist college, got married, and did good things, but I stopped pursuing a real relationship with Christ. You know there's a big difference in believing in Jesus as your Savior and living for Jesus because He saved you.

"I was spiritually very dry. I was as dry as a bone. And then while I was expecting my daughter Katie, things started to fall apart. There were severe problems, a lot of stuff. And that's when I turned to God, because there was nobody else to turn to; there was nobody else who could help. Nobody could make it better.

"I went in my bedroom and fell flat on my face. I remember it as clear as a bell. I said, 'All my life I've believed in You because I've been taught to believe in You, but this is one time when I am saying save me—physically, emotionally, spiritually. There is nowhere else to go. And if You are really the answer, then You have to show me now. I will know it, I will believe it. I'll never doubt it again. You have to get me to a place where I can function and get me through this situation.'

"I cannot begin to tell you the mercy and the grace that God poured out on us. He used people in our church, our Sunday school class, friends...but more than anything else I had this hunger for His Word that I had never had before. I mean, I had read my Bible before, I had taught Sunday school before, but never had I wanted to read it like I wanted it now. And never had I felt such a comfort from it. It was like I couldn't get enough. I've never doubted since then; I know beyond a shadow of a doubt Jesus is real, and He can get you through anything.

But it's quite possible to grow up in the church, believe in God, teach Sunday school, but really do it under your own steam. Because you're smart, you've got resources, training, self-confidence. We can pull off pretty good stuff for God, to a point. But at that point you only get human results; you don't get God-sized results.

Tell me about Moms in Touch. I know it's very important to you.

Well, my college roommate came to visit about three years ago, and at lunch we were talking about public school—the upside and the downside. My husband and I were trying to decide what to do about my son Will. I was scared; this was my first child going into public school. Amy asked if I'd ever heard about Moms in Touch, and I hadn't."

"She said, 'It's great. A bunch of us get together once a week. We pray for the school, for the children, for the teachers. We pray that godly principles will be taught there, pray for protection, pray that they will want to learn. We meet very casually. It's one hour to

"Do not be anxious about anything, but in everything, by prayer and petition, with thanksgiving, present your requests to God. And the peace of God, which transcends all understanding, will guard your hearts and your minds in Christ Jesus" (Phil 4:6–7).

Are you as anxious as the rest of the world? Or do you have peace about you that only comes through prayer?

commit to pray. You don't dress up, you don't eat food, you just pray for the school.'

"It did sound really great. So after Amy left, I was walking around the block that afternoon, and my neighbor Julia Halford came out of her house. She said, 'Pam! I am so glad you're walking by; I need to talk to you. Something has been on my heart. I don't know why God has given me your name, but I've been praying about this. Have you ever heard of Moms In Touch?'

"This was one of the those times when God sent me a neon sign! And I said, 'Not until about 15 minutes ago.' Julia said, 'You're kidding. Well, that must be why I'm supposed to talk to you about it. I really would like to start a group for Liberty Elementary School, but I don't know who else to talk to. I wondered if you would want to pray with me. Maybe we could get one started.'

"So Julia and I started meeting. It was the most wonderful experience. We'd get together for an hour—very casual, not a big deal—but leave with this wonderful peace about our children, the school, their teachers, about being a mom. It was incredible."

What would you pray for?

Well, we would pray that as mothers, we would have patience and joy and not want to pull our hair out.

We'd pray that we'd not get so wrapped up in volunteering that we'd forget what was important. We would pray that our children would be safe at school, that they would have a desire to learn, to do their best. We'd pray for their friends. One of the neatest things we prayed for was that our children would accept Christ at an early age. I prayed especially for Will that year. At the end of the year, he was asking a lot of questions about salvation. I was able to share the plan of salvation with my son, and the next morning he said, 'I prayed that prayer. I asked Jesus to come into my heart; I'm saved, and I want to be baptized.' And I did the same thing my mother did!

"Well, I didn't say 'you're not old enough,' but I was thinking it! I had been praying all year that he would accept Christ—and I got my answer! But I couldn't see that until Julia and I met, and then it hit me: I've been praying for this all year with this woman, and look what happened! It was just wild.

"I can't explain it, but when you pray with another person for an hour and empty out your heart—especially about your children and about being a mom—when you lay it all out on the line, there's this closeness. You bond very deeply."

Do you talk about it with each other, or do you just pray?

"You do not have because you do not ask God" (James 4:2).

Do you need power, peace, direction? Have you asked for it?

You just pray. It's hard!"

It is hard. Usually we get together for prayer groups, and we spend most of the time talking about our prayer requests—and then just say a five-minute "Lord, answer all these requests."

It's very easy to fall into that. There have been times when we'd get together and we'd talk; and we'd stop ourselves and say, 'We've got to pray.'"

Maybe that's why we lack power, we lack the things you've described—the peace, clear answers—because we don't go to God with our problems, we go to each other about them and say, "God, we hope you heard this."

Exactly. If we just had taken them to Him to begin with! And I still fall into that with all kinds of things: take it up, don't take it out.

"We found out we were moving to Atlanta. So I said, 'Just pray that somebody down there will want to pray with me through Moms in Touch. This is a new school. I don't know any of the teachers, and I'm nervous.' So I got there, and I didn't know if Will's teacher was a Christian, but I talked to her and said, 'I want to start this prayer group called Moms in Touch, but I don't know how the principal would feel about it. What do you think?' And she said, 'Oh, she is the strongest Christian. Phyllis will want you to do this.' So I thought, 'I'll give her a call.'

"Well, when I ran into her in the hall at school one day, she gave me the name of someone else that was interested in starting a group. She said, 'There are four or five people that want to be in this group, but they don't have a place to meet.' Isn't that wild? So we ordered the books and we got together."

Then, when you came back here from Atlanta, did you have to start over?

I was talking to another mom at school whose son is in Will's class, telling her about Moms in Touch, and she said, 'There's a mother in your neighborhood who wants to do that, too.' That mother, Robin, just happens to live right next door to me! And now we have a list of 10 people that want to participate."

We shouldn't be so amazed, should we? That's the way God intends for life to be; that's how He works. One reason we don't recognize miracles, or the power of God doesn't seem to manifest itself in our lives, is that we don't live at that level. We don't look for it and ask for it.

We don't ask. There have been times I have asked specifically, and I know I have seen God answer prayers that I never dreamed He would answer in such an incredible way. And you'd think I'd learn to take everything to Him, but I'm still surprised. I still

"Remain in me, and I will remain in you. No branch can bear fruit by itself; it must remain in the vine. Neither can you bear fruit unless you remain in me" (John 15:4).

Have you taken one step, spoken one word, considered one thought on your own without God?

have to remind myself: take it up, don't take it out."

Jennifer Kennedy Dean

As an author, speaker, and co-founder of The Praying Life Foundation, Jennifer Kennedy Dean has become a voice constantly reminding us to "take it up, don't take it out." Through her books, *Heart's Cry: Principles of Prayer*, *The Praying Life: Living Beyond Your Limits*, *Power Praying: Prayer That Produces Results*, and *Riches Stored in Secret Places*, Jennifer teaches us that prayer is a relationship rather than an activity.

Jennifer, what can I learn from Jesus' relationship to His Father?

To be as totally dependent upon the indwelling life of Christ as Jesus, in His earthly years, was dependent upon the Father. Not one word spoken, not one action taken, not one thought developed except in surrendered obedience.

"The danger in trying to be Christlike is that we will set up a list of 'Christlikeness rules' for all to follow. We humans are so drawn to hard and fast rules. This takes away the need for moment-by-moment dependence upon the present power of the Spirit. We can follow the rules, or we can follow the Ruler.

"When we use the formulized approach that goes along the lines of

'What would Jesus do?' we get into trouble. You know why? Because two honest Christians can honestly disagree on what Jesus would do! One might say, 'He'd always tell the truth, no matter how brutal.' Another might say, 'No... He'd be gentle and let the truth emerge.' Each would have a valid theological argument and could find a case in point from Scripture. We don't have to wonder what Jesus would do if He were here. He is here! We have to say, 'Jesus, what are You doing, and what do You want to do through me?' As long as Jesus is an outside figure whose example we should follow, we will never know power!"

You seem to me to have a lot of personal power. You are a gifted, visionary, intelligent woman. Are you telling me you don't rely on any of that?

It took several years for the Father to wean me from my confidence in my own ability to lead and influence others. I began to use my skills for Him, and it was successful and gratifying, but there was always this pestering thought: 'There's more.' The deeper His work went in me, the deeper I wanted to see it go in others. I found that I could not come up with the words (my reliable tools, in which I put much trust) that would speak the depths of what I knew. My greatest strength became one of my weaknesses.

"Then I discovered the secret: it is

"My grace is sufficient for you, for my power is made perfect in weakness." (2 Cor. 12:9).

What do you consider your greatest strengths? Have you acknowledged that they are not enough? Have you offered your weaknesses to the Lord? Do people see only your abilities, or do they marvel at what God can do in your weaknesses?

my weakness He wants! He can never display His power in my strength. He has to have my weakness. I was so determined to use my strengths for God that I panicked when I realized that my strengths were not strong enough...that I could never be satisfied with what my strengths, finely honed as they were, could produce. Instead of working to make them stronger, I had to recognize them as weakness and abandon them altogether. I had to come to the point where I would tremble at the prospect of having nothing but my own words to offer. I came to know that my words, no matter how cogently and skillfully arranged or how well delivered...my words can produce only momentary effect. Only God's words filled with God's power will produce change."

Okay, then, how does God give me His power?

God does not give me power. He exercises His power through me.

"What is power? It is the ability to produce the desired effect. Any action that does not produce the desired effect is powerless. So power can only be defined in the context of the desired effect. If my goal is to get attention, then I have power. If my goal is to impart information about God or the Bible, then I have power. But if my goal is to see people encounter God for themselves, or to see people changed by words of life, then I am powerless.

Only He has the words of life. I don't think that phrase means 'the words *about* life.' Jesus said, 'The words that I have spoken to you are Spirit and they are life' (John 6:63). His words have life in them and produce life in others."

Is prayer the source of that power?

No. God Himself indwelling me through His Spirit is the source of the power—but prayer is how the power is accessed. Prayer causes an ongoing interaction between the material realm and the spiritual realm. Prayer is what brings the power of heaven into the needs of earth.

"Prayer is happening when I am continually open to the Life that indwells me. So sometimes prayer takes the form of asking for what God longs to give; other times it takes the form of obedient action empowered by the Spirit; other times prayer is my God-ward thoughts; yet other times prayer is His thoughts toward me. That flow of His Life through my spirit-veins—that which keeps me abiding in Him—that's prayer. That's the key to how the power flows through me into the world. When His desired outcome has become my desired outcome, I will be totally dependent on His power."

Esther Burroughs

My favorite story about Esther Burroughs involves catching a plane. Esther

"It does not, therefore, depend on man's desire of effort, but on God's mercy. For the scripture says to Pharaoh; 'I raised you up for this very purpose, that I might display my power in you and that my name might be proclaimed in all the earth.'" (Rom. 9:16–17).

Why does God exercise His power through us? Not to accomplish our agendas, but to accomplish His.

"After they prayed, the place where they were meeting was shaken. And they were all filled with the Holy Spirit and spoke the word of God boldly" (Acts 4:31).

is always catching a plane. For almost 17 years, she worked with the Southern Baptist Home Mission Board (now part of the North American Mission Board) promoting evangelism for women. A riveting speaker and writer, she now travels constantly to speak at women's conferences and retreats. She is a gifted storyteller, and many of the experiences she shares are airplane stories.

On this occasion, she was chasing down a connecting flight in the Atlanta airport, and was running so late that she was driven right out on the tarmac, in between the huge planes, to arrive at her gate. As Esther tells it, she was rushed to her seat and strapped in as the doors slammed shut and the engine revved. As the plane backed away from the gate, Esther took a deep breath and sighed out loud, "Thank you, Father."

The man sitting next to her turned and asked, 'What are you, a nun?"

"No," Esther replied, "I'm a priest."

A fundamental tenet of Southern Baptist belief is the doctrine of "the priesthood of the believer": that every believer is empowered by God to accomplish His work through the Holy Spirit. *Empowered* is a big word in Esther's vocabulary. She spends a lot of time teaching women how the Holy Spirit has empowered them to be priests. On a summer afternoon in the hills of a North Carolina conference center, we sat in rockers on the porch of my cabin and talked about the Holy Spirit, power, and, of course, planes.

One of the passions I feel about women, and I feel from women, is they desire an intimacy with God, and they don't have any idea how to get it. They run from retreat to retreat and seminar to seminar. They're groupies, and they follow speakers. And they give away a power to the speaker that is available to every single one of us: the power that comes from knowing God intimately. *Any* woman that develops an intimacy with God—the overflow is her witness. It's natural; she can't stop it.

"Coming up here, I got on the airplane, and when I stepped on, both flight attendants standing there said, 'We love your dress! And your jewelry—we love your silver jewelry. You look like a million dollars!'

"I said with a smile, 'Thank you. I needed that today; you just blessed me.' And then I took my seat.

"We got up in the air, and this flight attendant came up, and she said, 'You're Esther Burroughs, the evangelist, aren't you?' I've never been asked that! I said, 'Yes I am.'

"She said, 'Just the way you spoke to us, I said to the other stewardess, "There's just a presence about her." '

"This woman knelt down, and she said to me, 'That's what the world needs is that presence of Christ in us that they can feel.'"

"But you are a chosen people, a royal priesthood, a holy nation, a people belonging to God, that you may declare the praises of him who called you out of darkness into his wonderful light" (1 Peter 2:9).

Do you think of yourself as a "lay person" or a "priest"? How does this affect your actions and attitudes?

"My soul thirsts for God, for the living God. When can I go and meet with God?" (Psalm 42:2).

Do you have that thirst? Then begin the discipline and pray for the thirst to follow.

How do you get that, Esther?

It's a discipline. You put becoming more like Christ on your list and it's the first thing you do in the morning. If you're not a morning person, plan to spend time with God when the energy is there for you—a meaningful time to meet the Father. And what happens is that when you find a tool like *My Utmost For His Highest* or *Streams in the Desert*, it gives you a little story and helps you look at the Word of God. I always say don't look at the Scripture in the devotional book; read the Scripture in the Word, because it's God-breathed. So when Oswald Chambers takes me to Isaiah, I turn to chapter 60. I can't take my eyes off the page, because up here in chapter 59, God tells me something else. I start crying, and before I ever get back to what Oswald had to say, I know God's faithfulness; I know this is a book of promises, and I can stand on it and go back to it. You stand on it and you sit on it and you write on it.

"See, Karla, if I can lead women to read the Word of God and God's Spirit breathes it to them, then they go, 'He gave this to *me!* He doesn't just give it to Esther!' and they start standing on it. When they themselves get in the Word, and it becomes theirs—not Karla's, not Esther's—God Himself puts a thirst there. And the five minutes spent with God becomes twenty and twenty an hour.

"So it's a discipline, and then the

thirst for it comes and the love comes, and then they begin to realize that they have the same power as He. Not as me or you, but as Christ, because He empowers us through the Spirit. We don't teach people enough about the Holy Spirit. We have no power without Him and no gifts without Him."

Maybe we don't teach the Spirit because He's bigger than we can control, I think.

He is. And He's a person. And we don't teach that He's a person. One time when I was speaking at a conference I said, 'If you only know the work of God the Father and God the Son, you only have two thirds of the power.' And this woman stood up and said, 'No, honey, you ain't got *no* power!' And I said, 'Oh, sister, you're right.' Nobody brings anybody to Christ but the Holy Spirit. He's ahead of us. He's behind us. He's within us. He's working in our lives; He's working in the person that doesn't know Him.

"I was leading a hotel maid to the Lord once. I said, 'Has anybody ever talked to you about Christ?' She said, 'No. Would you?' and I said, 'Maybe we should ask your supervisor if we can talk.' She said, 'We don't have to. She's already been praying for me.' See what just happened?"

"My Father is always at his work to this very day, and I, too, am working" (John 5:17).

Everywhere you go, God has already been there at work before you! How does that change the way you see your everyday activities?

"So neither he who plants nor he who waters is anything, but only God, who makes things grow" (1 Cor. 3:7).

Remember, it's only up to you to plant, water, or harvest. God will take care of the rest. Does that lift a burden off your shoulder?

Esther makes the whooshing sound of a wind blowing. I get goose bumps.

The wind blows wherever it pleases (John 3:8).

Yeah. The Spirit already had her supervisor there. I didn't plant any seeds; I wasn't part of anything except the harvest. And that's humbling because it's God's field."

And when you know that, then it's not as scary because it's not up to you.

It isn't up to you! It takes this huge burden off of you—and what you do is, you become a woman who lives in the expectancy of God's surprises. You know this because you get to the grocery store, and there's that woman in front of you, and you can just see her shoulders, weighed down. So you just play with her children and get her through the check-out line. What she feels is the breath of God.

"Another time when I was on an airplane, I was sitting by this woman, and we started talking, which always leads to, 'What do you do?'

"She said, 'I work with women's health issues,' and I said 'That's incredible; tell me about it.'

"Finally she asked, 'What do you do?' and I said, 'Well, I work with women's health issues, too.'

"She said, 'No kidding, who do you work for?'

"I said, 'Well I am a speaker; I travel and share with women about the most personal relationship that I have, and that's with Jesus.'

"She said, 'My soul!' and she grabbed me. She said, 'Wait!' and she reached in her purse and pulled out the pamphlet *Peace With God.*

"She said, 'Last week a man sat in that very chair, and he told me the very same thing. You don't think this is an accident, do you?'

"See what God did?"

Esther and I spontaneously "whoosh" together. My goose bumps return.

There really is a fragrance about us in every circumstance. And you can't be around a woman that is full of the Spirit of God that doesn't live on God's surprises and what God's going to bring her way. It's in the air around her.

"I tell stories like that to women and they say, 'I've never done anything like that!' They think they can't, that it wouldn't happen to them. One of my missions is to say, 'It's waiting to happen to *you*! Because you were created for one purpose, and that's to bring glory to the Father.' And I try to tell them to live in the expectancy of what God will do."

"Elijah was a man just like us. He prayed earnestly that it would not rain, and it did not rain on the land for three and a half years. Again he prayed, and the heavens gave rain, and the earth produced its crops" (James 5:17–18)

If it can happen to Elijah, it can happen to you! Do you believe that?

"But thanks be to God, who always leads us in triumphal procession and through us spreads everywhere the fragrance of the knowledge of him. For we are to God the aroma of Christ among those who are being saved and those who are perishing. To one we are the smell of death; to the other, the fragrance of life" (2 Cor. 2:14–16).

¹Phillips, J.B., *Your God Is Too Small* (New York: Macmillan, 1961).

9
Passion
Developing a Heart for God

One of them, an expert in the law, tested him with this question: "Teacher, which is the greatest commandment in the Law?" Jesus replied: "Love the Lord your God with all your heart and with all your soul and with all your mind" (Matt. 22:35–37).

When my husband, Dennis, and I were first married, we lived in a tiny apartment in what surely must be the armpit of Texas. We had one table, two chairs, a sofa, and a small television that got three channels (not even local). We both worked two jobs. We had one frying pan and about 18 casserole dishes (wedding gifts), and we ate pork chops and green peas almost every night, because that was about all I knew how to cook.

I thought I was in heaven. I just loved that man so much, I didn't care where I was as long as I was with him.

That is how God intends for us to love Him. "I will give them a heart to know me," He said to the prophet Jeremiah, "for they will return to me with all their heart" (Jer. 24:7). God is not content with half-hearted devotion. Jesus demonstrated for us what a life consumed with love for the Father looks like. A half-hearted love would not have compelled Him to the cross.

At revival services, we used to sing an old hymn that said, "Set my soul afire, Lord." I don't think we really meant it. I'm not even sure we understood what we were asking.

"I consider everything a loss compared to the surpassing greatness of knowing Christ Jesus my Lord," wrote Paul. "I consider them rubbish" (Phil. 3:8). "Any of you who does not give up everything he has cannot be my disciple," said Jesus in Luke 14:33. That's the kind of whole-hearted passion that sets your heart and soul on fire. Everything else pales in comparison. You love Him so much, you don't care where it leads, as long as you're with Him.

Betty Wiseman

She squirms when you ask her to talk about herself. I've been with Betty Wiseman in foreign countries when she was unafraid to talk with anybody, from palace guards to teenage gang members, but on the subject of Betty Wiseman she is far from comfortable. What Betty loves to talk about is God, and she will talk to anyone who will listen.

Betty Wiseman graduated from high school in 1961 with a contract to play semi-pro basketball. At the last minute she changed her mind and decided to go to Belmont College in Nashville, Tennessee, where she led the first women's collegiate basketball team in the state. In 1966, Betty joined Belmont's Health and Physical Education (HPE) faculty and became coach of the women's basketball and tennis teams. She coached six All-Americans, leading the 1979 and 1981 basketball teams to championships. Four times she was honored as Coach of the Year in her conference. In 1984, Betty retired from coaching, although she remained on the HPE faculty. In 1997, she became the Associate Athletic Director and Senior Women's Administrator at Belmont University.

Five years earlier, in 1992, Betty had discovered what would become her passion: sports evangelism. On almost every summer, spring, and winter break, you will find Betty somewhere overseas, usually toting Bibles and basketballs. She has traveled to Chile, Scotland, Poland, and Costa Rica. On many of those trips, she has taken a team of Belmont athletes with her.

Betty, tell me about your passions.

There was a time when I thought Belmont University couldn't do without me and as a basketball coach I was so intense. It does that to you; you're driven. My passions were caught up in where I was and my work. That doesn't mean that God wasn't important in my

"I have much more to say to you, more than you can now bear" (John 16:12).

God knows your heart. He knows if you are ready to obey what He tells you. Are you ready to hear what He has to say?

life, and I think through the years I've been able to be a witness, but I'd never been consumed with God. And it's like, 'Whoa! Why couldn't I have discovered this a long time ago?' But I think you have to be ready. It's your readiness to receive. If you're not ready for this in your life, God's not going to give it to you because He knows that you're going to mess it up. You wouldn't know what to do with it.

"I remember telling my friends who were visiting that summer I first went to Chile, (and this was prophetic) 'I don't know what it is, but I feel like I'm about to begin a whole new phase of my life.' They have reminded me many times of that. I don't know, I guess I was just ready for it; I had gotten burnt out on teaching.

"The first time I came back from a mission trip my heart was aching. It was like a whole world had opened up to me. God had just unzipped me and said, 'Okay, Betty this is what it's all about; this is what I've been preparing you for.' And I couldn't get in my mind what all this meant. I began to process. I cried. I felt uncomfortable back here. I just fell in love with God's world, these people. It's interesting the first place I ever went overseas was poor, poor, poor. Our family wasn't poor by any means, but we were poor folks growing up. And God put me among people just like I was growing up."

When did you become a Christian?

In April, when I was eleven years old. It was during a revival service that I asked Jesus into my heart, and I remember I couldn't wait until the next day to get to school and tell my teacher and my friends. You know? That was so important. And I was so happy and nothing really spectacular took place; I just knew that something happened in my heart that night. I just remember the joy of that night, and I'll never forget it, how excited I was—that I couldn't wait to tell somebody. I have remembered that on occasions as I have gotten more and more involved in missions—the joy of telling somebody. When we lose that joy, or don't have that joy of sharing, I think we miss out on what it's all about. It's not meant to be put inside and kept to ourselves."

How did you get your joy back?

I think the joy came back when God took me to another country and got me away from the boundaries of my life. You see, I had gotten trapped in this wilderness because of some of the needs I had for responsibility. I had taken the burden on myself. I took all the responsibility and that was a pattern in my life. And so, I left it all behind, things that I controlled, things that I was responsible for, things that had become a burden and a trap. I didn't realize that I needed to be freed from the controlling of those things. I started teaching

"No eye has seen, no ear has heard, no mind has conceived what God has prepared for those who love him" (1 Cor. 2:9–10).

You can't imagine what God has planned just ahead for you! Does that scare you? Is it exciting?

stress management about 10 years ago, and I began this class when I was under great stress. And I realize God put that in my life, because I learned a lot. I learned about control and the fact that we all want control in our lives. We want to control people; we want to control circumstances and things; we want to be in control of our lives. And there are certain things that we can have control over, but if you ask yourself, 'Can I fix it?' or 'Can I have some influence?' and the answer is no, then you'd better drop it.

"I let go of a lot of things, and I let Christ take control of my life unlike I ever had. As I look back I see how God really had a plan for my life. I can write a story about how that plan has unfolded. Everything that happened to me has happened for a purpose—it was very necessary and normal to bring me where I am. And I think, "Wow! You've been in control all along!" And now I'm so excited about tomorrow—what tomorrow's going to bring—because I know Who's in control. I don't worry about the future."

Tell me about your first trip to Chile. When did you go?

August 1992. That was my first overseas experience. I was scared to death! But it was there that God showed me for the first time how really simple the gospel is, sharing the gospel. How important my love is to people—the spontaneity of my love, who I am. And people sense that—people overseas, people here at home. It gave me a great sensitivity to opportunities here. I think that's what happened to me the most: God showed me how to be real, just be me and to share His love through that. To be with people and reach out, cry with them—I've shed a lot of tears when I couldn't communicate with them in South America and Poland and other places. But I knew that our hearts met.

You know? There's something about two hearts meeting that breaks down all barriers. You can't talk, but you can smile and hug and love through your eyes, your sensitivity. I'm just amazed at how Christ can use our bodies and our spirits. It's not us that reaches out to people. It wasn't me in Chile that first time. But I just got a glimpse of the world through God's eyes, and that world is not overseas always, it's right here beside us."

I was in Akron, Ohio, this past Easter, performing with a local choir and other guest soloists in an outstanding work called "Saviour." The soloists were staying at a hotel downtown, right on a nice public square that was the perfect place for walking. So I would take my portable cassette player out there and rehearse my part by listening to the tape as I walked. The square was enclosed on all sides by huge corporate buildings like First National Bank, Ohio Gas, Merrill Lynch, and so on.

"For God so loved the world that he gave his one and only Son, that whoever believes in him shall not perish but have eternal life" (John 3:16).

Think about how much God loves the people all around you. See them through His eyes.

One day, during the lunch hour, the square was full of employees from these buildings taking their lunch break. As I walked, I listened to the section of the music in which the lyrics say, "The kings of the earth and the kingdoms built by men | Rise up in their glory and go back to dust again."[1] I realized that I was literally walking among the kingdoms built by men! And then a song came on that said, "This must be a cross of love for God to bruise His only Son."[2] And I saw these people through God's eyes: oppressed, weary, misguided, unaware of their need. I felt His compassion for them. I really wanted to run up to someone and say, "God loves you!" And you know me; you know that is quite a stretch.

But, Betty, I shrank from that experience. I didn't want to see the world through God's eyes; His passion is too much for me.

I think when I discovered this passion—and that's one of my favorite words—my heart changed. I remember I would be singing in my own simple way (I would be mostly with women's groups that time), and I would see a woman listening, and we would make a connection somehow. I'm singing 'How Great Thou Art'—that's a universal song, we all know it—and I'm singing in English, she's hearing it in Spanish in her own way, and we have a connection. Tears are flowing, and I'm saying "God if you are this powerful..." I never knew

the power of Jesus' love before. I think
I knew it in my own heart, but I'd never
seen it as powerfully as I did down
there.

"I remember being out with the
Mapuchi Indians as far out as you possibly can go...Indians coming, walking
out of the hills to this little one-room
church. They have the service in the
afternoon because they don't have
lights. So I get up, and they want to
know who I am and ask me to sing. I
began singing this same song, and I
remember the faces of those Mapuchi
Indians who had never seen me
before...and the Spirit that was present
in that church—the power and the tears.
I asked them to join me. They were
singing in Mapuchi language, the missionaries were singing in Spanish, and
there I was leading in English.

"When we finished, I just asked one
of the missionaries to translate for me. I
said 'Here I am so far away from home,
and I've never seen your faces, but the
Spirit of Christ is so evident here.' I told
them how much I loved them and that I
was able to love them because of what
Christ had done in my life, because He
loved them. There was a worship experience there; it wasn't anything other
than the power of the Holy Spirit, what
God was able to do. That's one thing I
learned more than anything else: the
power of the Spirit in our lives. I think
that's why I'm able to stop and spontaneously worship. I look out this window often, just in a spirit of worship."

*That was Betty's first taste of the mis-
sions field. As I write this, she is in Costa
Rica with a team of students from Belmont University. She keeps going back.*

You know, I was on sabbatical, and I
had all these plans to do some
research in sports history and visit halls
of fame. But God was saying, 'Go back,
go back.' And I began to think 'What
am I going to do when I go back? What
do You want me to do?' He would
answer, 'Do what you do here. Those
kids need basketballs, beanbags, hula
hoops, and parachutes.' So I began saying to the university, 'Is it possible for
me to change my plans?' I began col-
lecting equipment. I made arrangements
with Clara Brincefield (my missionary
contact in Chile) to go back down there,
and I said, 'What can I do?'

'Just come, just come,' she said. So I
took this equipment, and I went and
worked in after-school programs, did PE
classes for kids, played with them and
held basketball clinics."

Same thing you do here.

Same thing. You know, that's what
God wants us to do, to use our
skills—as simple as it is in sports and
basketball, things I've been doing in
sports all my life, teaching PE—with

other people where it's needed, around the world. That's how He's going to use you. I hooked up one time with a medical clinic that was coming to Chile, and I worked with this medical team for two weeks down there and saw them first-hand. See, I teach health—I teach world health, health problems of the world—and I've been able to use that in my classes. It's almost mind-boggling to think about where God has taken me and brought me back home. As a result, here I am relating to these college students, and God is saying to me, 'Teach them to use their gifts for My glory **now**, so they don't wait until they are 40 to start.'

"God's given sports back to me, and now it's a ministry. See how that's evolved? He's given it back, and He's saying, 'Now, do something really meaningful.' The one thing I've tried to do is keep these kids that I take on mission trips involved in sharing the message that we should be using our gifts to minister."

Do the students experience the same thing you do on these trips?

The same thing, yes. Their minds are blown, and for some it's more meaningful than others. It serves a purpose in each one's life. I see it right down to every kid that went this year. We've had conversations about it, and I help them process what this means…changing majors as a result of

what they've discovered on this trip,
learning how to share their faith, and
how to be more open with it in their
own personal lives and relationships.
Being willing to stand up, like Kevin
Fields, a Belmont basketball team
player. He delivered the Baccalaureate
address at his high school two weeks
ago. That wouldn't have happened if
God hadn't prepared him through all
these times of sharing—and I'm still not
sure that God hasn't called him to the
ministry. He doesn't know it yet!

"But I think the thing that's happened
more than anything else is that I'm more
sensitive to opportunities on a daily
basis for ministry in my teaching, in
whatever I do. It may just mean recog-
nizing that when somebody comes to
my door, being conscious of the fact
that this may be Christ Himself. And
that's my prayer every morning when I
go to school: 'Reveal Yourself some way
to me today and help me receive You.'
So, if somebody comes to the door,
although I may be busy, to push back
and say, 'Come on in.' They sit down
and have something that is really important on their minds, and they need to
talk about it. And in some cases, before
it's over, I'll say, 'Would you like to pray
about it?' You can just see them going,
'Yeah, I'd like that,' with a sigh of relief.
So we close the door, and I hold their
hand and pray.

"Prentis McGoldrick, our former associate pastor, taught me that. He said 'I
dare you to pray, to ask God to show

you Himself in this day. And when He does, don't forget to thank Him.' Well, from that day on, I began practicing that: 'Show Yourself to me.' You expect it, and you acknowledge it. That's when it becomes so real. Sometimes when students walk out the door, I'll just smile and say, 'God, you're awesome!'"

That's an Old Testament practice. When Moses encountered the burning bush, he built an altar to say "God was here!" I don't think we celebrate enough when we bump into God. But it's a good thing for us to say, "Wow, thank You. You were here, and I saw it."

And the more you do that, the more you realize that you could have that 'wow' all the time. Sometimes when I stop to pray, I just begin with 'Wow, God!' I did that one time with a group, and when I finished, somebody said, "That's the first time I heard anybody say, 'Wow, God!' But that's worship. I'm a simple person, and that's just a simple way of saying it. He knows what I mean. And so I have a lot of 'wows' during the day.

"I think of all the missed opportunities through the years—missed in terms of opportunities for God to shine. But see, I wasn't ready for that kind of ministry. I just went down to visit a friend in Florida, and I thought, 'I'm going to take this video of our trip to Poland, and if I have a chance to be a witness, I will.' So, we had three people in—pro-

"You will seek me and find me when you seek me with all your heart" (Jer. 29:13).

Take Betty's challenge: Ask God to show Himself to you today. And when He does, don't forget to thank Him.

"For we cannot help speaking about what we have seen and heard" (Acts 4:20).

Are you excited about God? Do people know that just by your conversation?

fessors down there—and we were eating, very informal, and they started asking about my experiences, very intrigued because they're in a totally different ball game. I shared some things, and finally they wanted to know what in the world is sports evangelism? What do you do? And God was saying, 'Betty you can be bold.' So I said, 'I just happen to have a video, just 20 minutes; I'd be glad to share it with you.' They just jumped at it, so we all went in the den.

"I had to run downstairs and get it, so as I was coming back up, I just stopped on the stairs and said, 'God, this is it. This is Your time to shine.' Well, when one professor who was not a Christian left that night, she said, 'I have a lot to go home and think about—the things I've seen and heard about tonight.' When I went to bed I prayed for her and continue to pray for her. I just plant a seed; that's what I've learned."

Whatever you're passionate about, it's going to come up, wherever you are. If you're passionate about the Cowboys, you're going to talk about the Cowboys. Jesus could be at dinner, and the conversation turned to God because that was His passion. And people want to hear other people talk about their passion. It's a matter of talking about what you know and are excited about.

When they recognize that there is something different in your life, a student will come in and say, 'Professor

Wiseman, do you have just a few minutes?' They stammer and stutter and finally say, 'Somebody told me that you are a Christian and you will listen to me.' So the word gets out, and then it's expected of you. That changes my whole concept of why I'm here. I'm not here just as a teacher anymore; it's a calling for me, a ministry."

You know, Betty, you're going down the same career path you've been going down for years, but now you're going down it with a different perspective. You could have gone down it all this time and not seen God.

Not that I didn't serve a purpose all those years...but God can do so much more when your passion is for Him and not for what you're doing."

Saralu Lunn

My first memory of Saralu Lunn was by a campfire at a Sunday school party. Somebody started singing choruses—old choruses that we used to sing as kids—and Saralu was just going at it like a cheerleader, clapping along, her face radiating. And I thought, "How can she not be self-conscious?" I've been outspoken about God since I was kid, but to show my emotions is hard for me. So I was really impressed that Saralu could just let her absolute love for God beam out like that.

Saralu Lunn is a "beamer." Whatever

she is feeling, it beams in her face, times ten. We tease her about it, but it is one of the things I love best about my long-time friend. I admire the whole-hearted expression of her passion for God. But she explained to me that she didn't always have that kind of passion for God.

Oh! Karla, you did not know me when I had little kids. Life had to really change for me, or I was going to lose everything. So you didn't see me before. Well, I got to where I was because of what I had chosen. I go back, and I think what would I have done differently? Hopefully I would have done things differently.

"I was saved at six years old, and it was in the arms of my mother. I was in the church nursery with my mother, and I remember crawling up in my mother's lap and saying, 'Mom, I really want to ask Jesus into my heart.' And she said, 'You can do that right now.' I remember praying, and we walked out and told the preacher. And he had already dismissed the service, and he said, 'Everybody come back.' And I really believe that is exactly when I asked Jesus into my heart."

Saralu's family is like family to me. Her mother was a wise and deeply spiritual woman. Saralu's husband, Ed, is my husband's oldest and closest friend.

*Her children, Leigh Marie and Eddie,
are like my own. She has told me the
story of how Eddie was born, a gorgeous
boy with a huge, red birthmark covering
half his face—and what a turning point
that was for her.*

It was not until Eddie's birth that I had
to come face-to-face with the fact that
there was either a God up there Who
had made no mistakes, or I was going
to hang it up. Because to me, church
was just a social thing. Yes, I was a
Christian and went to church. I was very
legalistic.

"Our first child, Leigh Marie, was born
a "Gerber baby." But Ed was born two
years later with the birthmark on his
face. I knew he would carry my attitude
the rest of his life. I knew that either
God had not made a mistake with
Eddie, and He knew exactly what He
was doing, or my faith was not worth it.
I remember struggling for six months
with that baby. I would look at people
that I knew had something different
than I did, and I could not figure out
what they had, but I knew I didn't have
it. And I would cry out. And being that
legalistic, I would go to the Scripture
and I would read, and it would mean
nothing to me. I would get on my knees
and pray...and *nothing.* I could not figure out how I could get it. I knew there
was something I was missing.

"I remember falling on my knees one
night by the side of my bed and just

"Why are you
downcast, O
my soul? Why
so disturbed
within me? Put
your hope in
God, for I will
yet again praise
Him . . ."
(Psalm 42:11).

Have you ever
wondered if
God had made
a mistake? How
did you
respond?

"If you call out for insight and cry aloud for understanding, and if you look for it as silver and search for it as a hidden treasure, then you will understand the fear of the Lord and find the knowledge of God" (Prov. 2:3–6).

Do you need to understand God? This is His promise to you.

crying out, 'God, I don't know how You can be anymore to me than what You are, but if You say You are Lord of my life, I'm going to believe it, and I'm going to accept it.' It was like scales being removed from my eyes. I could not get enough of God's Word. It just came alive to me. I absolutely fell in love with God's Word. I got into every Bible study I could possibly get into.

"And what God did was put such love in my heart for my son that for the next few years, it seemed that God anointed everything Eddie did."

The birthmark, by the way, has not hindered that handsome kid from snagging every beautiful girl he sees, or from being a leader among his peers. Several years ago, when offered the option of a laser procedure that could possibly remove the mark, Eddie chose to keep it.

When you look back now, and he's almost completely grown, can you see a purpose in that birthmark? Other than bringing you to God.

Well, that's the main thing—for me. Every time I look at that birthmark I know that brought my change. I would not have been the mother I should be if that had not happened. My personality's happy-go-lucky-everything's-great; and that's exactly the way I would've lived my life. I probably would have had a much easier marriage. But I would not have felt the urgency to talk to my family about how Christ had changed my life."

Why do you say your marriage might have been easier?

I think it was because there was such a dramatic change in my life—that passion because I was experiencing such spiritual growth. I tried to share it with my husband, and what happened was that my husband, Ed, was going, 'You are not the woman that I married.'"

"He said: 'How do I compete with God?'"

Well, Saralu, you did get very churchy for awhile.

Oh, extremely! Volunteer everything. I just went to the far extreme. And Ed was busy building a company. He went this way, and I went that way for eight years. And finally he rebelled and said, 'I'm not taking this anymore. I love you but I can't live with you.' I look back, and I think, 'Gosh, I did it so wrong because I almost lost my marriage.'

"What scares me about people who become passionate for ministry and for working for God is that's what you do, you work for God. And what happens is that usually your family suffers for it."

"If anyone does not provide for his relatives, and especially for his immediate family, he has denied the faith and is worse than an unbeliever" (1 Tim. 5:8).

There is more to "providing" than just physical needs; there are also emotional and spiritual needs. Are you shortchanging your family? God's word is harsh, but clear.

"Create in me a
pure heart, O
God...You do
not delight in
sacrifice, or I
would bring
it...The sacri-
fices of God are
a broken spirit;
a broken and
contrite heart,
O God, you
will not
despise" (Psalm
51:10,16–17).

Is God bringing
you to your
knees to purify
your heart?

*I have a feeling there are a lot of kids
and men out there who've had it with
church work and everything else that
their wives are in.*

And that's what happened with us.
And thank God Ed rebelled. He
would say, 'I don't want you to change;
how could I take you away from God?' I
think he felt that God had taken me
away from him. But the fact is that I
had it all screwed up."

*Nobody would've thought that. Any
good church woman would think you
were doing it all right.*

Exactly. That is what is so phenomenal: that I looked on the outside like
I was doing it all right, but in reality I
was doing it all wrong. And what God
showed me....He absolutely took me
back to my knees for the next six years
and showed me His faithfulness. I had
all the knowledge up to then, but I did-
n't know God's faithfulness."

*You know what you did: you just got
up off your knees the first time and
replaced a relationship with the Lord,
which you'd ask for, with working for the
Lord.*

Exactly. Because that's what I had
always known—my mother had
always worked in the church. And that
came easier. That was the easiest thing."

I'm learning that love for God ultimately leads you to love others. It's not exclusive of people. In fact, if you fall in love with God, if you're passionate for God, if you have "a pure heart," then He will give you a greater capacity to love people. That's a sure sign. So if you're spending hours and hours devoted to God, and it's not making a difference in your relationships, then you're not on the right track.

And I sure wasn't. But those next years, God stripped away everything. Everything. I remember the only thing I could do when Ed would turn in the driveway—I would run to the window, and I would fall down on my knees because I couldn't express myself; I looked like a fumbling idiot. And what God showed me was that if I could just ask Him to help me do one little thing—be able to say, 'How was your day?'—little by little God showed me His faithfulness if I would just turn it over to Him. If I just let Him do it. And even though it was so hard for those six years, there was such joy to me because I was seeing God work through me even in an impossible situation.

"What God was doing was just stripping me of my security, and He was saying, 'Your security is in me. That is the only security you have.' Truly you look back, and you are thankful for every bit of that because of God's faithfulness. Because you actually saw God's faithfulness in everything."

"Not everyone who says to me, 'Lord, Lord,' will enter the kingdom of heaven, but only he who does the will of my Father who is in heaven. Many will say to me on that day, 'Lord, Lord, did we not prophesy in your name, and in your name drive out demons and perform many miracles?' Then I will tell them plainly, 'I never knew you'" (Matt. 7:21–23).

Busy–ness for God is not necessarily a sign of obedience to His will. What's important is that we hear what He tells us to do and obey only that. Activity is no substitute for a relationship with Christ.

"I waited patiently for the Lord; he turned to me and heard my cry. He lifted me out of the slimy pit, out of the mud and mire; he set my feet on a rock and gave me a firm place to stand. He put a new song in my mouth, a hymn of praise to our God. Many will see and fear and put their trust in the Lord" (Psalm 40:1–3).

Your testimony of God's faithfulness to you can inspire others to trust God. Can you point to God's faithfulness in a particular situation?

You need to know that Saralu Lunn has every reason to find her security elsewhere. She is a beautiful woman with style oozing out her pores. She has two gorgeous children, a marriage that is reborn and thriving, a successful business, an impressive and comfortable home, and a large circle of devoted friends. She would be the first to admit that she has been abundantly blessed, but Saralu puts no confidence in the blessings. Her heart belongs to the Giver. She has what the Psalmist David called "an undivided heart" (Psalm 86:11).

I'm basically a very selfish person. I really am. I'm self-centered; I have tunnel vision. And so I have to always come back to that place where I say, 'Make me pure in heart.' That's the basis of everything—what's in your heart. Every single day, I have to yield my heart to Him and say, 'Take my heart and make my desire to focus on You, not me.'"

If you and I were "beamers" like Saralu Lunn, what would our lives radiate? Our benefits from God? Our activity for God? Our performance enabled by God? Or would we glow with the presence of God?

We must simply love and surrender

ourselves to the person of God, above anything else in this world or the next, loving Him, even if there are no blessings. Yielding our hearts to Him, though He may not move mountains on our behalf. Content to sit with Him, with no assignment to do. This is a heart for God: loving Him so much that we don't care about anything else; we just want to be with Him. And that's enough.

"For the eyes of the Lord range throughout the earth to strengthen those whose hearts are fully committed to him" (2 Chron. 15:9).

[1]Farrell, Bob and Greg Nelson, "Kings of the Earth" (©1994 Gentle Ben Music/Dayspring Music/Summerdawn Music/Steadfast Music ASCAP).
[2]Farrell/Nelson, "Cross of Love" (©1994 Gentle Ben Music/Dayspring Music/Summerdawn Music/Steadfast Music ASCAP).

10

Jesus Lives Here

I no longer live, but Christ lives in me
(Gal. 2:20*a*).

Writing this book has changed my life.
It has shattered almost everything I
thought being a Christian was about. It
has shown me the mark—Jesus Christ—
and how far off the mark I am.

I began almost a year ago with a
smug, self-assured idea of what it meant
to be different. I had a list of outstanding women with impressive credentials,
many of whom have changed large
parts of the world. Andrea Mullins, my
friend and mentor at Woman's Missionary Union®, asked me, "Are these
women different because of what they
do, or are they different because Christ
lives in them?"

That was when I realized I hadn't a
clue, and began to get one very quickly.
Lifestyle evangelism is not so much
about being different because of the
things you *do*; it is about standing out
from your culture because of who you
are. It is not about activity; it is about
character. The goal of life is that "Christ
is formed in you" (Gal. 4:19).

Jesus is out there, walking around in
the world through the lives of believers,
like the women in this book. I know
some of them. So do you.

Helpful Hints

How do you and I become Christlike?

ᢓ᪲**Ask.** Pursue a witnessing lifestyle.
God wants to form Christ in us, not so
that we can be good people, but so that
others may see Him and be drawn to
Him. "I will do this," the Lord says, "not
for your sakes, but for the sake of my
reputation" (Ezek. 36:22, paraphrase
mine).

ᢓ᪲**Look for Christ.** If you ask Him,
expect Him to be there. As Esther Burroughs challenged us, live in the
expectancy of what God will do. Don't
look for an assignment; look for Him.

ᢓ᪲**Prioritize relationships, not activities.**
In fact, give up some activities, as Claire
Cloninger did, so that you are more
available to people and to Christ.
Remember that activity is not as impor-
tant to God as intimacy.

ᢓ᪲**Get to know Christ.** Read the
biographies of the four Gospels, not just
the just "how-to" of the Epistles. Spend
time getting to know Christ, His culture,
His nature. Learn to recognize His voice
and take on His way of thinking. Don't
pursue a set of directions. Pursue the
person of Christ. Invite Him into all the
rooms of your life.

We can offer our culture no less profound a witness than that. We must not
offer them a sanitized version of their

own values, nor a watered-down version of God's. They have seen both, and they are not buying it. Nothing short of the pure and wholehearted, life-changing habitation of Jesus Christ will persuade them. The world today does not need a Christian "sub-culture" any more than it did in the city of Antioch in the first century. Like those who have gone before us, we must become a counter-culture. We must be unswerving in our passion for the things which Christ loves, unflinching in our stand for the truths which Christ revealed, and unrelenting in our loving pursuit of those for whom He gave His life to redeem. Our lives must look like Him, walk like Him, talk like Him, and smell like Him—not just on Sundays, but Monday through Saturday, sunup to sundown. In our everyday going and coming, we must obey Him, remember Him, celebrate Him, and embody Him.

Jesus Lives Here

In the church, we speak of "living for Jesus." I think that misses the point. Living *for* Jesus implies that we are still trying to do something of our own effort on His behalf. It's still a "white-wash" job—all outward. As long as we concentrate on Christian activities, we do not necessarily show people what Christ looks like; we just show them what a busy Christian looks like.

Rather, it is about Jesus living *in* me. The apostle Paul said, "I've tried that checklist, busy-for-God thing, and it doesn't work" (Gal. 2:9, paraphrase mine). Then he described what does work: "I have been crucified with Christ *and I no longer live, but Christ lives in me*" (Gal. 2:20*a*, emphasis mine).

That's what Paul meant: See this life? I have moved out. Jesus lives here.

Lord Jesus, I have left You outside the door of my life. Forgive me. I hear You knocking, but I can't unlock the door on my own! Give me the key. Speak to me through Your Word; only You have the words of life. I want to fling wide the door of my heart and open all the windows. I want to let the breath of God blow in and the fragrance of Christ waft out. I want my neighbors, friends, and family to see that You have moved in. I want You to be evident everywhere I go, in whatever I do. I want to know You, to share the cup of fellowship. I know this will cost me; make me willing to drink the cup of sacrifice, if that's what You require. Lord, I yield my life to You—this day and everyday. Come into my heart, Lord Jesus. Make my heart Your home. Amen.